Mike McGrath

C Programming

fifth edition

In easy steps is an imprint of In Easy Steps Limited
16 Hamilton Terrace · Holly Walk · Leamington Spa
Warwickshire · United Kingdom · CV32 4LY
www.ineasysteps.com

5th Edition

Printed and bound in the United Kingdom

ISBN 978-1-84078-840-2

Contents

1	**Getting Started**	**7**
	Introducing the C language	8
	Installing a C compiler	10
	Writing a C program	12
	Compiling a C program	14
	Understanding compilation	16
	Summary	18
2	**Storing Variable Values**	**19**
	Creating program variables	20
	Displaying variable values	22
	Inputting variable values	24
	Qualifying data types	26
	Using global variables	28
	Registering variables	30
	Converting data types	32
	Creating array variables	34
	Describing dimensions	36
	Summary	38
3	**Setting Constant Values**	**39**
	Declaring program constants	40
	Enumerating constant values	42
	Creating a constant type	44
	Defining constants	46
	Debugging definitions	48
	Summary	50
4	**Performing Operations**	**51**
	Doing arithmetic	52
	Assigning values	54
	Comparing values	56
	Assessing logic	58
	Examining conditions	60
	Measuring size	62
	Comparing bit values	64

Flagging bits 66
Understanding precedence 68
Summary 70

5 Making Statements 71

Testing expressions 72
Branching switches 74
Looping for a number 76
Looping while true 78
Breaking out of loops 80
Going to labels 82
Summary 84

6 Employing Functions 85

Declaring functions 86
Supplying arguments 88
Calling recursively 90
Placing functions in headers 92
Restricting accessibility 94
Summary 96

7 Pointing to Data 97

Accessing data via pointers 98
Doing pointer arithmetic 100
Passing pointers to functions 102
Creating arrays of pointers 104
Pointing to functions 106
Summary 108

8 Manipulating Strings 109

Reading strings 110
Copying strings 112
Joining strings 114
Finding substrings 116
Validating strings 118
Converting strings 120
Summary 122

9 Building Structures 123

Grouping in a structure 124
Defining type structures 126
Using pointers in structures 128
Pointing to structures 130
Passing structures to functions 132
Grouping in a union 134
Allocating memory 136
Summary 138

10 Producing Results 139

Creating a file 140
Reading & writing characters 142
Reading & writing lines 144
Reading & writing entire files 146
Scanning filestreams 148
Reporting errors 150
Getting the date and time 152
Running a timer 154
Generating random numbers 156
Displaying a dialog box 158
Summary 160

+ Reference Section 161

ASCII character codes 162
Input & output functions 164
Character test functions 173
String functions 174
Math functions 176
Utility functions 178
Diagnostic functions 180
Argument functions 180
Date & time functions 181
Jump functions 184
Signal functions 184
Limit constants 185
Float constants 186

Index 187

Preface

The creation of this book has provided me, Mike McGrath, a welcome opportunity to update my previous books on C programming with the latest techniques. All examples I have given in this book demonstrate C features supported by current compilers on both Windows and Linux operating systems, and the book's screenshots illustrate the actual results produced by compiling and executing the listed code.

Conventions in this book

In order to clarify the code listed in the steps given in each example, I have adopted certain colorization conventions. Components of the C language itself are colored blue; numeric and string values are red; programmer-specified names are black; and comments are green, like this:

```
/* Store then output a text string value. */
char *myMessage = "Hello from C" ;
printf( myMessage ) ;
```

Additionally, in order to identify each source code file described in the steps, a colored icon and file name appears in the margin alongside the steps:

main.c

header.h

Grabbing the source code

For convenience I have placed source code files from the examples featured in this book into a single ZIP archive, which you can obtain by following these easy steps:

1. Browse to **www.ineasysteps.com** then navigate to Free Resources and choose the Downloads section

2. Find C Programming in easy steps, 5th edition in the list, then click on the hyperlink entitled All Code Examples to download the archive

3. Now, extract the archive contents to any convenient location on your computer

I sincerely hope you enjoy discovering the powerful expressive possibilities of C programming and have as much fun with it as I did in writing this book.

Mike McGrath

1 Getting Started

Welcome to the world of C. This chapter demonstrates how to create a C program in text, then how to compile it into executable byte form.

8 Introducing the C language
10 Installing a C compiler
12 Writing a C program
14 Compiling a C program
16 Understanding compilation
18 Summary

Introducing the C language

Dennis M Ritchie, creator of the C programming language.

C is a compact, general-purpose computer programming language that was originally developed by Dennis MacAlistair Ritchie for the Unix operating system. It was first implemented on the Digital Equipment Corporation PDP-11 computer in 1972.

This new programming language was named "C" as it succeeded an earlier programming language named "B" that had been introduced around 1970.

The Unix operating system and virtually all Unix applications are written in the C language. However, C is not limited to a particular platform and programs can be created on any machine that supports C, including those running the Windows platform.

The flexibility and portability of C made it very popular and the language was formalized in 1989 by the American National Standards Institute (ANSI). The ANSI standard unambiguously defined each aspect of C, thereby eliminating previous uncertainty about the precise syntax of the language.

ANSI C has become the recognized standard for the C language and is described, and demonstrated by examples, in this book.

Why learn C programming?

The C language has been around for quite some time and has seen the introduction of newer programming languages like Java, C++, and C#. Many of these new languages are derived, at least in part, from C – but are much larger in size. The more compact C is better to start out in programming because it's simpler to learn.

Programs written 20 years ago in C are still just as valid today as they were back then.

It is easier to move on to learn the newer languages once the principles of C programming have been grasped. For instance, C++ is an extension of C and can be difficult to learn unless you have mastered C programming first.

Despite the extra features available in newer languages, C remains popular because it is versatile and efficient. It is used today on a large number of platforms, for everything from micro-controllers to the most advanced scientific systems. Programmers around the world embrace C because it allows them maximum control and efficiency in their programs.

Standard C libraries

ANSI C defines a number of standard libraries that contain tried-and-tested functions, which can be used in your own C programs.

The libraries are contained in "header files" that each has a file extension of ".h". The names of the standard C library header files are listed in the table below with a description of their purpose:

Library:	Description:
stdio.h	Contains input and output functions, types, and macro definitions. This library is used by most C programs and represents almost one third of the entire C libraries
ctype.h	Contains functions for testing characters
string.h	Contains functions for manipulating strings
math.h	Contains mathematical functions
stdlib.h	Contains utility functions for number conversion, storage allocation, etc.
assert.h	Contains a function that can be used to add diagnostics to a program
stdarg.h	Contains a function that can be used to step through a list of function arguments
setjmp.h	Contains a function that can be used to avoid the normal call and return sequence
signal.h	Contains functions for handling exceptional conditions that may arise in a program
time.h	Contains functions for manipulating date and time components
limits.h	Contains constant definitions for the size of C data types
float.h	Contains constant definitions relating to floating-point arithmetic

A function is a piece of code that can be re-used repeatedly in a C program. A description of each function in the C library is given in the Reference section starting on page 161.

Installing a C compiler

C programs are initially created as plain text files, saved with a ".c" file extension. These can be written in any plain text editor such as Windows' Notepad application – no special software is needed.

"GNU" is a recursive acronym for "Gnu's Not Unix" and it is pronounced "guh-new". You can find more details at www.gnu.org

In order to execute a C program it must first be "compiled" into byte code that can be understood by the computer. A C compiler reads the original text version of the program and translates it into a second file, which is in machine-readable executable byte format.

If the text program contains any syntax errors these will be reported by the compiler, and the executable file will not be built.

One of the most popular C compilers is the GNU C Compiler (GCC) that is available free under the terms of the General Public License (GPL). It is included with almost all distributions of the Linux operating system. The GNU C Compiler is used to compile all the examples in this book into executable byte code.

To discover if you already have the GNU C Compiler on your system, type **gcc -v** at a command prompt. If it is available the compiler will respond with version information:

When a C compiler is installed the standard C library header files (listed on the previous page) will also be installed.

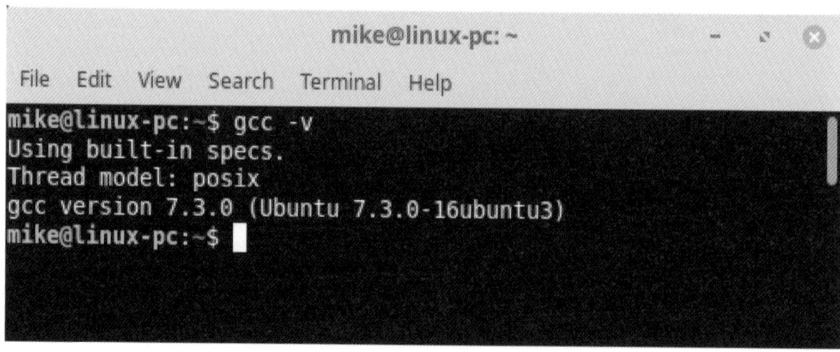

mike@linux-pc: ~
File Edit View Search Terminal Help
mike@linux-pc:~$ gcc -v
Using built-in specs.
Thread model: posix
gcc version 7.3.0 (Ubuntu 7.3.0-16ubuntu3)
mike@linux-pc:~$

If you are using the Linux operating system and the GNU C Compiler is not available, install it from the distribution disk or online repository, or ask your system administrator to install it.

If you are using the Windows operating system and the GNU C Compiler is not already available, you can download and install the Minimalist GNU for Windows (MinGW) package, which includes the GNU C Compiler, by following the steps opposite.

...cont'd

1. With an internet connection open, launch a web browser then navigate to **sourceforge.net/projects/mingw** and click the "Download" button to get the MinGW setup installer

2. Launch the setup installer and accept the suggested location of **C:\MinGW** in the "Installation Manager" dialog

3. Choose the "Basic" and "C++ Compiler" items then click **Installation**, **Apply Changes** to complete the installation

MinGW Installation Manager

Installation Package Settings Help

Basic Setup
All Packages

	Package	Class	Installed Version	Repository Version	Description
☐	mingw-developer-tool...	bin		2013072300	An MSYS Installation for MinGW Developers (meta)
☑	mingw32-base	bin		2013072200	A Basic MinGW Installation
☐	mingw32-gcc-ada	bin		6.3.0-1	The GNU Ada Compiler
☐	mingw32-gcc-fortran	bin		6.3.0-1	The GNU FORTRAN Compiler
☑	mingw32-gcc-g++	bin		6.3.0-1	The GNU C++ Compiler
☐	mingw32-gcc-objc	bin		6.3.0-1	The GNU Objective-C Compiler
☐	msys-base	bin		2013072300	A Basic MSYS Installation (meta)

Because C++ is an extension of C any C++ development tool can also be used to compile C programs.

The MinGW C++ Compiler is a binary executable file located at **C:\MinGW\bin**. To allow it to be accessible from any system location this folder should now be added to the System Path:

4. In Windows' Control Panel, click the **System** icon then select the **Advanced System Settings** item to launch the "System Properties" dialog

5. In the System Properties dialog, click the **Environment Variables** button, select the **Path** system variable, then click the **Edit** button and add the location **C:\MinGW\bin;**

6. Click **OK** to close each dialog, then open a "Command Prompt" window and enter the command **gcc -v** to see the compiler respond with version information

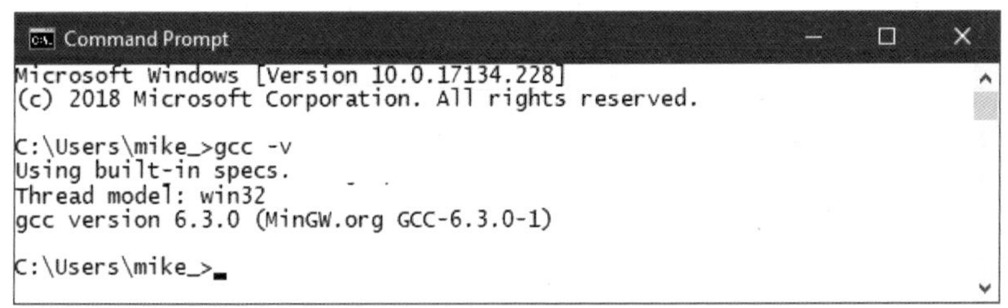

```
Command Prompt
Microsoft Windows [Version 10.0.17134.228]
(c) 2018 Microsoft Corporation. All rights reserved.

C:\Users\mike_>gcc -v
Using built-in specs.
Thread model: win32
gcc version 6.3.0 (MinGW.org GCC-6.3.0-1)

C:\Users\mike_>
```

Location addresses in the Path statement must end with a **;** semi-colon.

Edit System Variable

Variable name: Path

Variable value: C:\MinGW\bin;

The MinGW installation process may be subject to change, but current guidance can be found at **mingw.org/wiki/Getting_Started**

Writing a C program

Do not use word processor applications to create program code as they store additional formatting information that prevents code compilation.

In C programs the code statements to be executed are contained within “functions”, which are defined using this syntax format:

***data-type function-name* ( ) { *statements-to-be-executed* }**

After a function has been called upon to execute the statements it contains, it can return a value to the caller. This value must be of the data type specified before the function name.

A program can contain one or many functions but must always have a function named “main”. The **main()** function is the starting point of all C programs, and the C compiler will not compile the code unless it finds a **main()** function within the program.

Other functions in a program may be given any name you like using letters, digits, and the underscore character, but the name may not begin with a digit. Also, the C keywords, listed in the table on the front inner cover of this book, must be avoided.

Preprocessor instructions begin with a **#** hash character and must enclose standard library names within **< >** angled brackets.

The **( )** parentheses that follow the function name may, optionally, contain values to be used by that function. These take the form of a comma-separated list and are known as function “arguments” or “parameters”.

The **{ }** curly brackets (braces) contain the statements to be executed whenever that function is called. Each statement must be terminated by a semi-colon, in the same way that English language sentences must be terminated by a period/full stop.

Traditionally, the first program to attempt when learning any programming language is that which simply generates the message “Hello World”.

hello.c

Open a plain text editor, such as Notepad, then type this line of code at the start of the page, exactly as it is listed **#include <stdio.h>**

The program begins with an instruction to the C compiler to include information from the standard input/output **stdio.h** library file. This makes the functions contained within that library available for use within this program. The instruction is more properly called a “preprocessor instruction” or “preprocessor directive” and must always appear at the start of the page, before the actual program code is processed.

2. Two lines below the preprocessor instruction, add an empty main function

```
int main()
{

}
```

This function declaration specifies that an integer value, of the **int** data type, should be returned by the function upon completion.

Whitespace between the code is ignored by the C compiler but program code should always end with a newline character.

3. Between the braces, insert a line of code that calls upon one of the functions defined in the standard input/output library – made available by the preprocessor instruction

```
printf ( "Hello World!\n" ) ;
```

Here the **printf()** function specifies a single string argument between its parentheses. In C programming, strings must always be enclosed within double quotes. This string contains the text **Hello World** and the **\n** "newline" escape sequence that moves the print head to the left margin of the next line.

4. Between the braces, insert a final line of code to return a zero integer value, as required by the function declaration

```
return 0 ;
```

Traditionally, returning a value of zero after the execution of a program indicates to the operating system that the program executed correctly.

Each statement must be terminated by a semi-colon character.

5. Check that the program code looks exactly like the listing below, then add a final newline character (hit Return after the closing brace) and save the program as "hello.c"

```
#include <stdio.h>

int main()
{
  printf( "Hello World!\n" ) ;
  return 0 ;
}
```

The complete program in text format is now ready to be compiled into machine-readable byte format as an executable file.

Compiling a C program

The C source code files for the examples in this book are stored in a directory created expressly for that purpose. The directory is named "MyPrograms" and its absolute address on Windows is **C:\MyPrograms**, whereas on Linux it's at **/home/*user*/MyPrograms**. The **hello.c** source code file, created by following the steps on pages 12-13, is saved in this directory awaiting compilation to produce a version in executable byte code format.

At a command prompt, type **gcc --help** then hit Return to see a list of all compiler options.

1. At a command prompt, issue a **cd** command with the path to the **MyPrograms** directory to navigate there

2. At a command prompt in the **MyPrograms** directory, type **gcc hello.c** then hit Return to compile the program

When the compilation succeeds, the compiler creates an executable file alongside the original source code file. By default, this file will be named **a.out** on Linux systems and **a.exe** on Windows systems. Compiling a different C source code file in the **MyPrograms** directory would now overwrite the first executable file without warning. This is obviously unsatisfactory so a custom name for the executable file must be specified when compiling **hello.c**. This can be achieved by including a **-o** option followed by a custom name in the compiler command.

3. At a command prompt in the **MyPrograms** directory, type **gcc hello.c -o hello.exe** then hit Return to compile the program once more

On both Linux and Windows systems an executable file named **hello.exe** is now created alongside the C source code file:

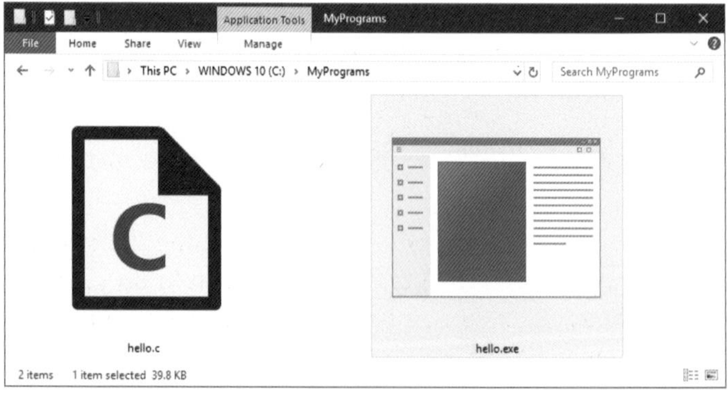

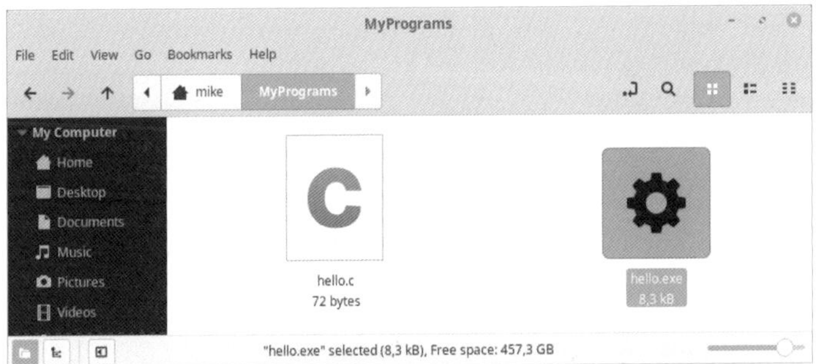

If the compiler complains that there is no new line at the end of the file add a carriage return to the end of the source code, then save and retry.

4. At a command prompt in Windows, type the executable filename then hit Return to run the program – the text string is output and the print head moves to the next line

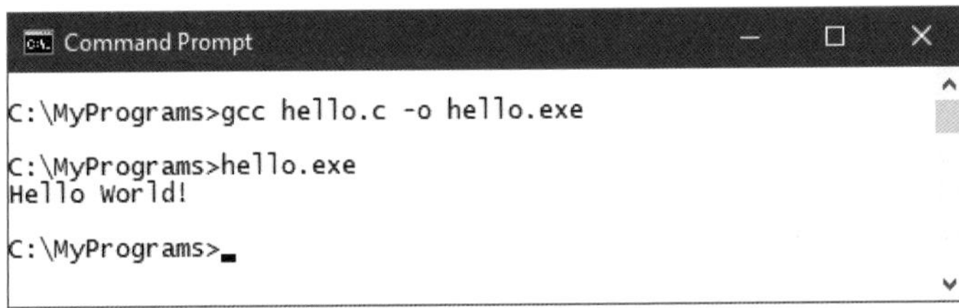

Because Linux does not by default look in the current directory for executable files, unless it is specifically directed to do so, it is necessary to prefix the filename with ./ to execute the program.

5. At a command prompt in Linux, type **./hello.exe** then hit Return to run the program – the text string is output and the print head moves to the next line

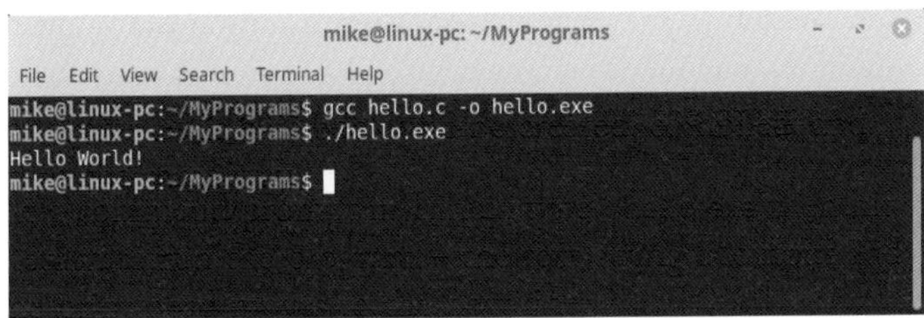

Windows users can even omit the file extension to run programs. In this case, typing just **hello** is sufficient.

You have now created, compiled, and executed the simple Hello World program that is the starting point in C programming. All other examples in this book will be created, compiled, and executed in the same way.

Understanding compilation

In producing an executable file from an original C source code file, the compilation process actually undergoes four separate stages, which each generate a new file:

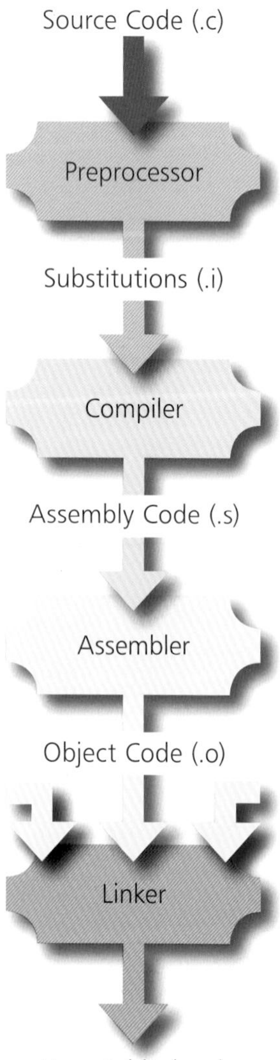

- Preprocessing – The preprocessor substitutes all preprocessor directives in the original source code **.c** file with actual library code that implements those directives. For instance, library code is substituted for **#include** directives. The generated file containing the substitutions is in text format and typically has a **.i** file extension.
- Translating – The compiler translates the high-level instructions in the **.i** file into low-level Assembly language instructions. The generated file containing the translation is in text format and typically has a **.s** file extension.
- Assembling – The assembler converts the Assembly language text instructions in the **.s** file into machine code. The generated object file containing the conversion is in binary format and typically has a **.o** file extension.
- Linking – The linker combines one or more binary object **.o** files into a single executable file. The generated file is in binary format and typically has a **.exe** file extension.

Strictly speaking, "compilation" describes the first three stages above, which operate on a single source code text file and ultimately generate a single binary object file. Where the program source code contains syntax errors, such as a missing semi-colon statement terminator or a missing parenthesis, they will be reported by the compiler and compilation will fail.

The linker, on the other hand, can operate on multiple object files and ultimately generates a single executable file. This allows the creation of large programs from modular object files that may each contain reusable functions. Where the linker finds a function of the same name defined in multiple object files it will report an error and the executable file will not be created.

Normally, the temporary files created during the intermediary stages of the compilation process are automatically deleted, but they can be retained for inspection by including a **-save-temps** option in the compiler command:

1. At a command prompt in the **MyPrograms** directory, type **gcc hello.c -save-temps -o hello.exe** then hit Return to recompile the program and save the temporary files

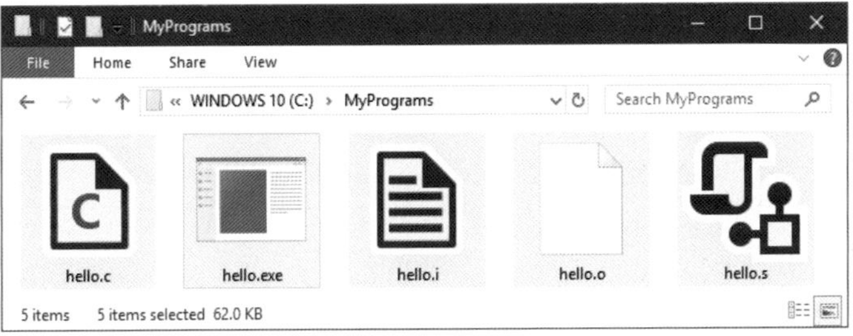

2. Open the **hello.i** file in a plain text editor such as Windows' Notepad, to see your source code at the very end of the file preceded by substituted **stdio.h** library code

3. Now, open the **hello.s** file in a plain text editor to see the translation into low-level Assembly code and note how unfriendly that appears in contrast to the C code version

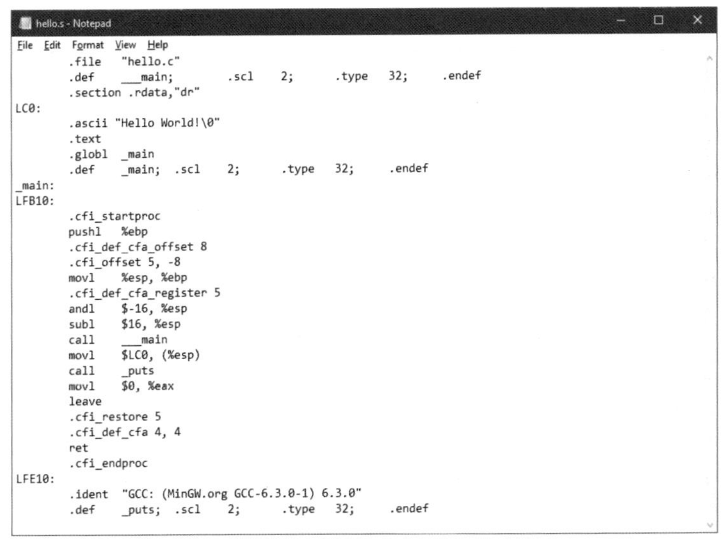


```
	.file	"hello.c"
	.def	___main;	.scl	2;	.type	32;	.endef
	.section .rdata,"dr"
LC0:
	.ascii "Hello World!\0"
	.text
	.globl	_main
	.def	_main;	.scl	2;	.type	32;	.endef
_main:
LFB10:
	.cfi_startproc
	pushl	%ebp
	.cfi_def_cfa_offset 8
	.cfi_offset 5, -8
	movl	%esp, %ebp
	.cfi_def_cfa_register 5
	andl	$-16, %esp
	subl	$16, %esp
	call	___main
	movl	$LC0, (%esp)
	call	_puts
	movl	$0, %eax
	leave
	.cfi_restore 5
	.cfi_def_cfa 4, 4
	ret
	.cfi_endproc
LFE10:
	.ident	"GCC: (MinGW.org GCC-6.3.0-1) 6.3.0"
	.def	_puts;	.scl	2;	.type	32;	.endef
```

Programs tediously written in Assembly language can run faster than those written in C but are more difficult to develop and maintain. For traditional computer programming, C is almost always the first choice.

Summary

- The American National Standards Institute (ANSI) established the recognized standard for the C programming language.
- Other programming languages, such as C++ and C#, are derived in part from the C language.
- The C language has a number of standard libraries containing tried-and-tested functions that can be used in any program.
- C libraries are contained in header files whose names have a **.h** file extension.
- C programs are created as plain text files whose names have a **.c** file extension.
- The popular GNU C Compiler (GCC) is included in the Minimalist GNU for Windows (MinGW) package.
- Adding the compiler's host directory to the system path conveniently allows the compiler to be run from any directory.
- Programs have one or more functions containing statements to be executed whenever the function is called.
- Every C program must have a **main()** function.
- A function declaration begins by specifying the data type of the value to be returned after the function has been executed.
- The statements to be executed are contained within **{ }** braces and each statement must end with a **;** semi-colon terminator.
- Preprocessor instructions are implemented in the first stage of program compilation and will typically substitute library code.
- The GNU C Compiler is run with the **gcc** command and may include a **-o** option to name the executable output file.
- Temporary files created during the compilation process can be retained using the **-save-temps** compiler command option.

2 Storing Variable Values

This chapter demonstrates how to store, retrieve, and manipulate various types of data using variable containers in C programs.

20 Creating program variables
22 Displaying variable values
24 Inputting variable values
26 Qualifying data types
28 Using global variables
30 Registering variables
32 Converting data types
34 Creating array variables
36 Describing dimensions
38 Summary

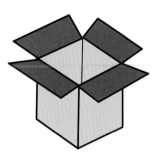

Creating program variables

A variable is a container in a C program in which a data value can be stored inside the computer's memory. The stored value can be referenced using the variable's name. The programmer can choose any name for a variable providing it adheres to the naming conventions listed in the table below:

Naming rule:	Example:
CANNOT contain any of the C keywords	**volatile**
CANNOT contain arithmetic operators	**a+b*c**
CANNOT contain punctuation characters	**%$#@!**
CANNOT contain any spaces	**no spaces**
CANNOT start with a number	**2bad**
CAN contain numbers elsewhere	**good1**
CAN contain mixed case	**UPdown**
CAN contain underscores	**is_ok**

Variable names are case-sensitive in C – so variables named "VAR", "Var", and "var" would be treated as three separate variables.

It is good practice to choose meaningful names for variables to make the program code more easily understood. To create a variable in the program simply requires it to be "declared". A variable declaration has this syntax:

data-type variable-name ;

C keywords are listed in the table on the inner front cover of this book.

First, the declaration specifies which type of data the variable is permitted to contain. This will be one of the four data types described on the opposite page. The data type is followed by a space then the chosen variable name, adhering to the naming conventions in the table above. As with all statements in C programs, the declaration must end with a semi-colon terminator. Multiple variables of the same data type can be created in a single declaration as a comma-separated list, like this:

data-type variable-name-1 , variable-name-2 , variable-name-3 ;

There are four basic data types in the C language. These are defined using the C keywords that are listed in the table below, together with a description of each data type:

Data type:	Description:	Example:
char	A single byte, capable of storing just one character	'A'
int	An integer whole number	100
float	A floating-point number, correct to six decimal places	0.123456
double	A floating-point number, correct to 10 decimal places	0.0123456789

Values of the **char** data type must always be enclosed by single quotes – double quotes are incorrect.

The four data types allocate different amounts of machine memory for storing data. The smallest is the **char** data type, which allocates just a single byte of memory; and the largest is the **double** data type, which typically allocates eight bytes of memory. This is twice the amount of memory allocated by the **float** data type so the **double** data type should only be used when a lengthy, precise floating-point number is a necessity.

Variable declarations should be made before any executable code appears in the program. When a value is assigned to a variable, that variable is said to have been "initialized". Optionally, a variable may be initialized when it is declared.

In a variable assignment the part to the left of the = operator is known as the L-value object and that to its right is known as the R-value data.

The example code fragment below declares and initializes various variables with appropriate values as described in the code comments – descriptive comments between /* and */ that are ignored by the compiler:

```
int num1 , num2 ;          /* Declares two integer variables. */

char letter ;              /* Declares a character variable. */

float decimal = 7.5 ;      /* Declares and initializes
                                         a floating-point variable. */

num1 = 100 ;               /* Initializes the integer variables. */
num 2 = 200 ;

letter = 'A' ;             /* Initializes the character variable. */
```

Displaying variable values

The value of variables can be displayed using the **printf()** function that was used in Chapter 1 to display the "Hello World" message. The desired format in which to display the variable value must be specified as an argument in the **printf()** function's parentheses using a suitable "format specifier", along with the variable name:

Specifier:	Description:	Example:
%d	An integer -32768 to +32767	100
%ld	A long integer -2^{31} to $+2^{31}$	123456789
%f	A floating-point number	0.123456
%c	A single character	'A'
%s	A string of characters	"Hello World"
%p	A machine memory address	0x0022FF34

Single **char** character values must be enclosed by single quotes – a string of multiple characters, on the other hand, must be enclosed by double quotes.

A format specifier can ensure that the output occupies a specific minimum number of spaces by stating the required number immediately after the **%** character – for example, to ensure that an integer always fills at least seven spaces with the specifier **%7d.** If it is preferable for the blank spaces to be filled with zeros just add a zero between the **%** character and the specified number – for example, to ensure that an integer always fills at least seven spaces and that blank spaces are filled with zeros with the specifier **%07d.**

A precision specifier, which is a period (full stop) followed by a number, can be used with the **%f** format specifier to determine how many decimal places to display – for example, to display just two decimal places with the precision specifier **%.2f.** The precision specifier can also be combined with the minimum space specifier to control both the minimum number of spaces and number of decimal places to display – for example, to display seven spaces including two decimal places and empty spaces filled by zeros with **%07.2f.**

By default, empty spaces precede the number so it is right-aligned, but can be added after the number to make it left-aligned by prefixing the minimum space specifier with a minus sign.

vars.c

1. Begin a new program with a preprocessor instruction to include the standard input/output library functions

```
#include <stdio.h>
```

2. Add a main function that declares and initializes two variables

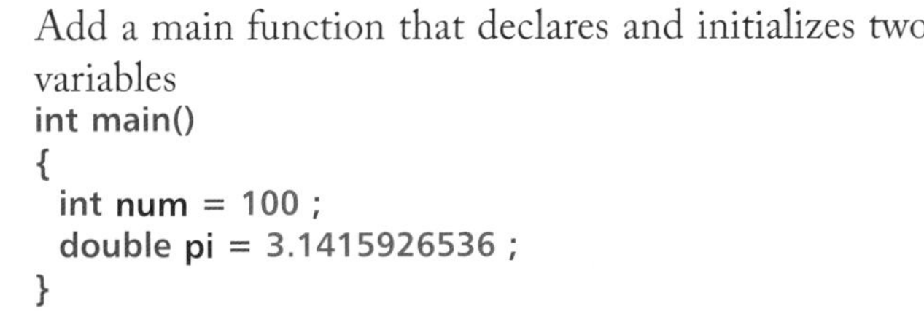

```
int main()
{
  int num = 100 ;
  double pi = 3.1415926536 ;
}
```

3. In the main function, after the variable declarations, insert statements to output the variable values in various formats

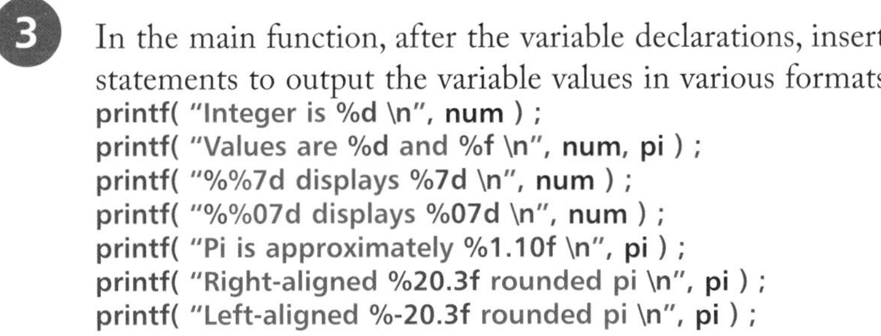

```
printf( "Integer is %d \n", num ) ;
printf( "Values are %d and %f \n", num, pi ) ;
printf( "%%7d displays %7d \n", num ) ;
printf( "%%07d displays %07d \n", num ) ;
printf( "Pi is approximately %1.10f \n", pi ) ;
printf( "Right-aligned %20.3f rounded pi \n", pi ) ;
printf( "Left-aligned %-20.3f rounded pi \n", pi ) ;
```

To display a "%" character with the **printf()** function, prefix it with another "%" character, as seen here.

4. At the end of the main function block, insert a final statement to return a zero integer value, as required by the function declaration

```
return 0 ;
```

Notice that the floating-point value is rounded when the format specifier allocates fewer decimal places – it is not simply truncated.

5. Save the program file then, at a command prompt, compile and execute the program to see the variable values be output in the specified formats

```
Command Prompt

C:\MyPrograms>gcc vars.c -o vars.exe

C:\MyPrograms>vars
Integer is 100
Values are 100 and 3.141593
%7d displays     100
%07d displays 0000100
Pi is approximately 3.1415926536
Right-aligned                3.142 rounded pi
Left-aligned 3.142                rounded pi

C:\MyPrograms>_
```

Inputting variable values

Strings are a special case and are demonstrated with the topic of arrays on page 34.

The standard input/output library **stdio.h** provides a **scanf()** function that can be used to get user input into a program. The **scanf()** function requires two arguments within its parentheses to specify the type of data to be input and the location where the input should be stored.

The first argument to the **scanf()** function must be one of the format specifiers from the table on page 22 between double quotes – for example, **"%d"** where input is an integer value. The second argument to the **scanf()** function must be a variable name preceded by the **&** character, except when the input data is a string of text. The **&** character has several uses in C programming but in this context is the "addressof" operator, which means that the input data should be stored at the memory location reserved for that variable.

When a variable is declared, space is reserved in the machine's memory to store the data assigned to that variable. The number of bytes reserved depends on the data type of the variable. The allocated memory is referenced by the unique variable name.

Envision the computer's memory as a very long row of slots. Each slot has a unique address, which is expressed in hexadecimal format. It's like a long road of houses – each house contains people and has a unique numeric address. In C programs the houses are the slots, and the people are the data contained in those addresses.

Note that the **scanf()** function stops reading input when it encounters a space.

The **scanf()** function can simultaneously assign values to multiple variables too. Its first argument must then contain a list of format specifiers, each separated by a space, and the entire list must be enclosed by double quotes. The second argument must contain a comma-separated list of variable names, each preceded by the **&** addressof operator, to which each specified format applies.

The **&** addressof operator can also be used to return the hexadecimal memory address at which the variable data is stored.

Combining output from the **printf()** function and input from the **scanf()** function creates basic interactivity between the user and the program.

setvars.c

1. Begin a new program with a preprocessor instruction to include the standard input/output library functions

```
#include <stdio.h>
```

2. Add a main function that declares three variables

```
int main()
{
  char letter ;
  int num1 , num2 ;
}
```

3. In the main function, after the variable declarations, insert statements to get input from the user

```
printf( "Enter any one keyboard character: " ) ;
scanf( "%c", &letter ) ;
printf( "Enter two integers separated by a space: " ) ;
scanf( "%d %d" , &num1, &num2 ) ;
```

4. Next, insert statements to output the stored data details

```
printf( "Numbers input: %d and %d \n", num1, num2 ) ;
printf( "Letter input: %c ", letter ) ;
printf( "  Stored at: %p \n", &letter ) ;
```

5. At the end of the main function block, insert a final statement to return a zero integer value, as required by the function declaration

```
return 0 ;
```

6. Save the program file; compile and execute the program; input data when requested; then see the stored data output

The format specifier for a machine address is **%p**.

Command Prompt

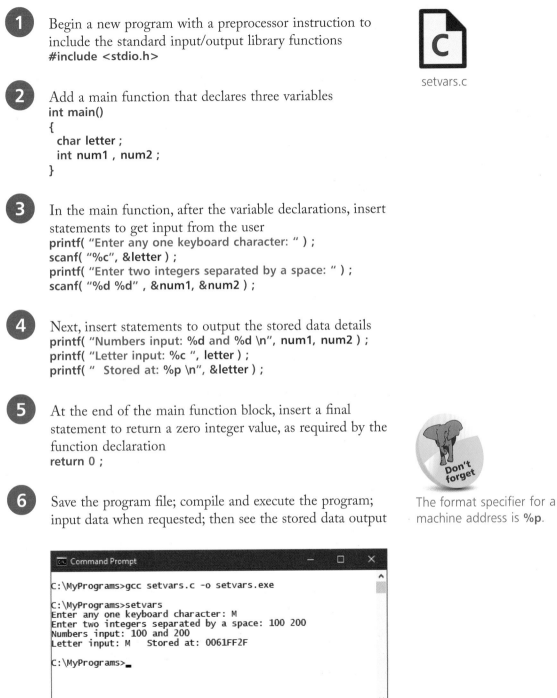

```
C:\MyPrograms>gcc setvars.c -o setvars.exe

C:\MyPrograms>setvars
Enter any one keyboard character: M
Enter two integers separated by a space: 100 200
Numbers input: 100 and 200
Letter input: M   Stored at: 0061FF2F

C:\MyPrograms>_
```

Qualifying data types

When an integer variable, of the **int** data type, is created it can by default contain either positive or negative values. These are known as "signed" values. The range of possible values is determined by your system as either "long" or "short".

Constants are always named entirely in uppercase to distinguish them from variables.

If the **int** variable is created by default as a long type (likely) it will typically have a possible range of values from a maximum of +2,147,483,647 down to a minimum of -2,147,483,648.

On the other hand, if the **int** variable is created by default as a short type (unlikely) it will typically have a possible range of values from a maximum of +32,767 to a minimum of -32,768.

The range size can be explicitly specified, however, using the **short** and **long** qualifier keywords in the variable declaration, like this:

```
short int num1 ;        /* Saves memory space. */

long int num2 ;         /* Allows bigger range. */
```

The **limits.h** C library header file contains implementation-defined limits for the size of each data type. These can be accessed via constant values named **INT_MAX** and **INT_MIN** for **int** variable declarations of unspecified size. Similarly, **SHRT_MAX** and **SHRT_MIN** contain limits for **short int** variable declarations, and **LONG_MAX** and **LONG_MIN** contain limits for **long int** variable declarations.

The memory space allocated to an **int** variable of unspecified size is system-dependent but will often be treated as a **long int** by default.

A non-negative "unsigned" **int** variable can be declared using the **unsigned** qualifier keyword when the variable will never be assigned a negative value. An **unsigned short int** variable will typically have a possible range from 0 to 65,535 but only occupy the same memory space as a regular **short int** variable. An **unsigned long int** variable will typically have a possible range from 0 to 4,294,967,295 but will only occupy the same memory space as a regular **long int** variable.

The C **sizeof** operator can be used to reveal the amount of memory space reserved by variables of different data types. It is good programming practice to use the smallest amount of memory possible. For example, where a variable will only ever contain positive integer values below 65,535 it is preferable to use an **unsigned short int** variable that reserves just 2 bytes of memory rather than a **long int** variable that reserves 4 bytes of memory.

sizeof.c

1. Begin a new program with a preprocessor instruction to include the standard input/output functions and constants

```
#include <stdio.h>
#include <limits.h>
```

2. Add a main function that contains statements to output the size and range of the **short int** data type

```
int main()
{
  printf( "short int... \tsize: %d bytes \t", sizeof( short int ));
  printf( "%d to %d \n" , SHRT_MAX , SHRT_MIN ) ;
}
```

3. Next, insert statements to output the size and range of the **long int** data type

```
printf( "long int... \tsize: %d bytes \t" , sizeof( long int ) ) ;
printf( "%ld to %ld \n" , LONG_MAX , LONG_MIN ) ;
```

4. Now, insert statements to output the size of other data

```
printf( "char... \tsize: %d byte \n" , sizeof( char ) ) ;
printf( "float... \tsize: %d bytes \n" , sizeof( float ) ) ;
printf( "double... \tsize: %d bytes \n" , sizeof( double ) ) ;
```

5. Insert a final statement to return a zero integer value, as required by the function declaration

```
return 0 ;
```

6. Save the program file, then compile and execute the program to see the data type sizes and ranges

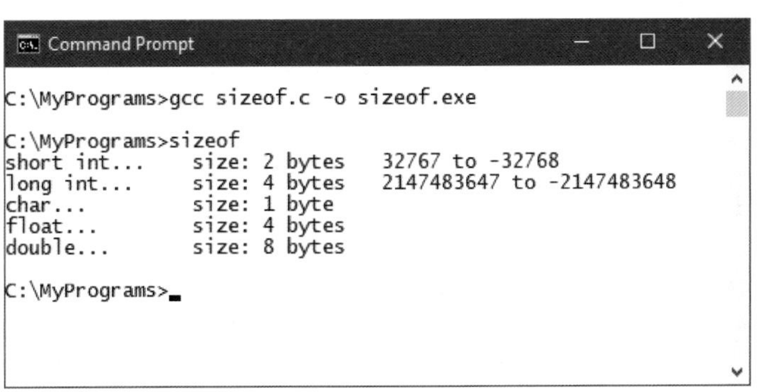

Command Prompt
C:\MyPrograms>gcc sizeof.c -o sizeof.exe
C:\MyPrograms>sizeof
short int...   size: 2 bytes   32767 to -32768
long int...   size: 4 bytes   2147483647 to -2147483648
char...   size: 1 byte
float...   size: 4 bytes
double...   size: 8 bytes
C:\MyPrograms>

Notice how the **\t** tab escape sequence is used in this example to space the output.

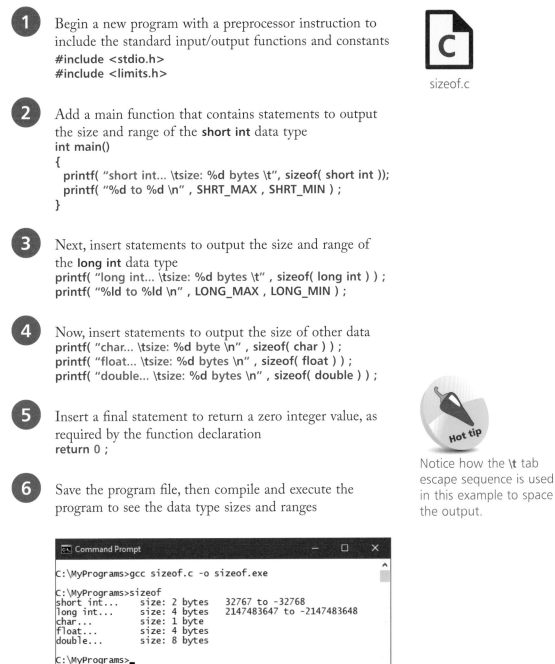

Using global variables

The extent to which variables are accessible in a program is called the "variable scope". Variables declared within a function are known as "local" variables, whereas variables declared outside any function blocks are known as "global" variables.

Local variables can only be accessed from within the function in which they are declared. This is the default implicit behavior that could be explicitly specified with the seldom-used **auto** keyword in the variable declaration. They come into existence when the function is called, and normally disappear when the function ends.

Global variables, on the other hand, can be accessed from within any function in the program. They come into existence when the program executes, and remain in existence until the program ends.

Widespread use of global variables can introduce name conflicts.

An external global variable must be defined exactly once at the start of the program. It must also be declared at the start of each function that needs access to it. The declaration should begin with the **extern** keyword to denote that it references an external variable, rather than a regular local variable declaration. These declarations should not be used to initialize the global variable.

Larger C programs often consist of multiple source code files that are compiled together to create a single executable file. Global variables are normally accessible from any function in any of the files being compiled together. All functions are normally accessible globally too, but functions and – more usually – global variables can have their accessibility limited to just the file in which they are created by the use of the **static** keyword in their declaration.

Try to use only local variables. Global variables allow convenient access to values from any function within a program but it is better practice to avoid global variables and pass values between functions as arguments instead.

Normally, a program cannot employ multiple variables of the same name but can do so if each is declared to be a **static** variable and is unique within that source code file. Programming with multiple source code files can reveal a common global variable name duplicated in two different files. Declaring these as **static** avoids the need to rename one of the variables in each occurrence within the source code.

Internal local variables can also be declared as **static**. These are only accessible from within the function in which they are declared, as usual, but they do not disappear when the function ends. This allows permanent private storage within a function until the program ends.

global_1.c

1. Begin a new program with a preprocessor instruction to include the standard input/output library functions
#include <stdio.h>

2. Define and initialize a global static variable that may only be accessed from within this source code file
static int sum = 100 ;

Adding the **static** keyword to the **num** variable definition in the second file would limit its accessibility to just that file – so compilation would then fail.

3. Add a main function that declares it wants to use the global static variable and output its value

```
int main()
{
  extern int sum ;
  printf( "Sum is %d \n" , sum ) ;
}
```

4. Now, insert a declaration to use a second global variable and output its value

```
extern int num ;
printf( "Num is %d \n" , num ) ;
```

5. Insert a final statement to return a zero integer value, as required by the function declaration, then save the file
return 0 ;

global_2.c

6. In a separate file define the second global variable, then save that file
int num = 200 ;

7. Compile both source files into one executable program, by supplying each source code filename in the command, then execute the program to see the global values output

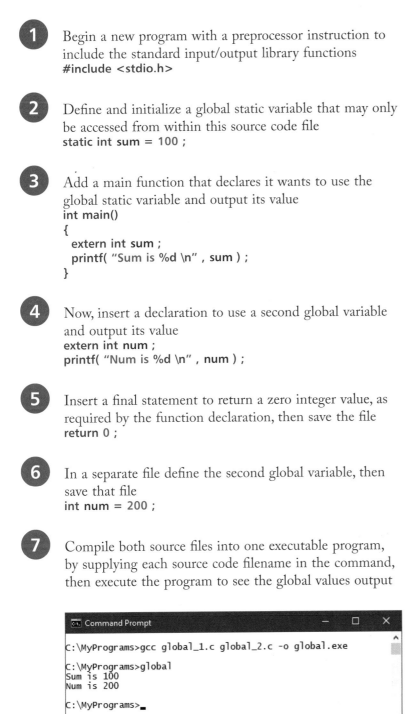

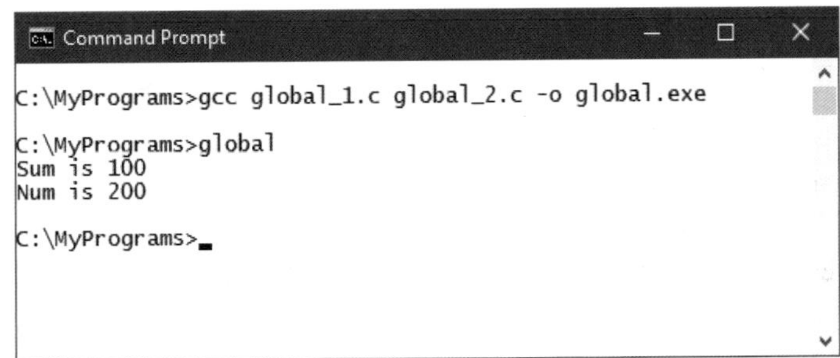

Command Prompt
C:\MyPrograms>gcc global_1.c global_2.c -o global.exe
C:\MyPrograms>global
Sum is 100
Num is 200
C:\MyPrograms>

Registering variables

A variable declaration that includes the **register** keyword advises the compiler that the specified variable will be heavily used by the program. The intention is for the compiler to place **register** variables in the machine registers of the computer to speed up access times. Their usefulness may be questionable, though, as compilers are free to ignore this advice.

Only local internal variables can be declared as **register** variables. In any case, only a few variables can be held in machine registers and they may only be of certain types. The precise limitations vary from machine to machine.

Despite these possible drawbacks, **register** declarations are harmless because the **register** keyword is ignored when the compiler cannot actually use the machine registers to store the variable. Instead, the variable is created as though the **register** keyword was not there.

The complete opposite of a **register** variable is achieved with a variable declaration that includes the **volatile** keyword. This means that the variable must not be stored in a machine register, as its value may change at any time without action being taken by any code the compiler finds nearby. This is particularly relevant to global variables in large programs that may be concurrently modified by multiple threads.

The **register** and **volatile** keywords are described here for completeness but are seldom found in reality as most programs simply use regular variables to store data.

One sort of variable that might benefit from being a **register** variable is a local variable used to store the control value of a loop. On each iteration of the loop, that value must be compared and changed so the variable is being repeatedly accessed. Storing this value in a machine register could then speed up execution of the loop.

On the other hand, if a global variable is used to store the control value of a loop and may also be changed from outside the loop, that global variable might benefit from being a **volatile** variable.

Loop structures are described fully in Chapter 5, but the example listed opposite is included to illustrate the repeated access of a **register** variable.

C

register.c

1 Begin a new program with a preprocessor instruction to include the standard input/output library functions

```
#include <stdio.h>
```

2 Add a main function that declares and initializes a local register variable containing a loop control value of zero

```
int main()
{
  register int num = 0 ;
}
```

3 Now, insert a conditional test to see if the control value is below five, followed by a pair of braces

```
while ( num < 5 )
{                                        }
```

4 Between the braces of the loop structure, insert statements to increment the control value and output its current value on each iteration of the loop

```
++num ;
printf( "Pass %d \n" , num ) ;
```

5 At the end of the function block, return a zero integer value, as required by the function declaration

```
return 0 ;
```

6 Save the program file, then compile and execute the program to see the values retrieved from the register variable on each iteration of the loop

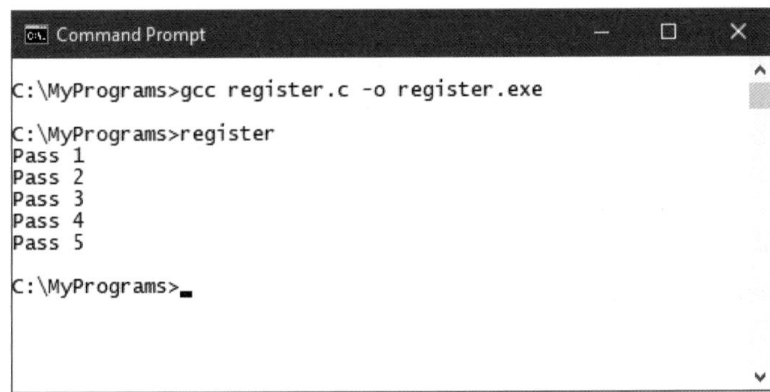
Command Prompt
C:\MyPrograms>gcc register.c -o register.exe
C:\MyPrograms>register
Pass 1
Pass 2
Pass 3
Pass 4
Pass 5
C:\MyPrograms>_

Beware

If the **&** addressof operator is used on a **register** variable the compiler will place the variable in a memory location rather than in a register.

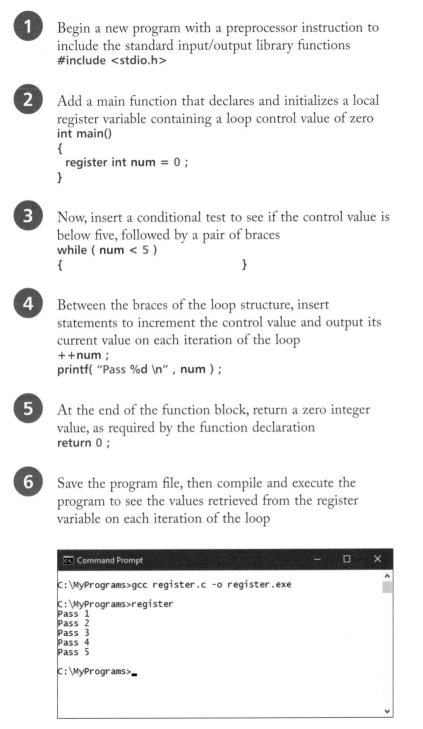

Converting data types

The compiler will implicitly change one type of data into another if it seems logical to do so. For example, where an integer is assigned to a **float** variable, the compiler converts the integer to a floating-point value.

ASCII (pronounced as "as-kee") is an acronym for "American Standard Code for Information Interchange" and is the accepted standard for plain text. You can find the full range of standard ASCII codes on pages 162-163.

Any data stored in a variable can be explicitly forced (coerced) into a variable of a different data type by a process known as "casting". A cast just states the data type to which the variable should be converted in parentheses before the name of the variable storing the data in its original data type. The parentheses should also include any modifiers, such as **unsigned**, where appropriate – so the syntax of a cast looks like this:

***variable-name2* = (*modifiers data-type*) *variable-name1* ;**

Note that casting does not change the original data type of the variable but merely copies that value as a different data type.

When casting from a **float** variable into an **int** variable the value is simply truncated at the decimal point. There is no rounding to the nearest integer. For example, with **float num = 5.75** the cast to an integer with **(int)num** produces the integer **5**, not **6**.

When casting from a **char** variable to an **int** variable the resulting integer value is the numerical ASCII code value that represents that character. The uppercase alphabet has numerical ASCII values 65-90, whereas the lowercase alphabet has 97-122. For example, with **char letter = 'A'** the cast to an integer with **(int) letter** produces the integer **65**. Casting integer values within these ranges to a **char** data type produces the equivalent letter.

The / forward slash character is the division operator in the C language.

It is often necessary to cast integer values into their floating-point equivalents to perform accurate arithmetic. Division can otherwise produce a truncated integer result. For example, with **int x=7,y=5** the statement **float z = x / y** assigns the value of **1.000000**. Accurate arithmetic requires the statement to use casts as **(float)x / (float)y** produces the floating-point value of **1.400000**.

Casting long, precise floating-point numbers from a **double** data type into a shorter **float** data type does not simply truncate the longer value at the sixth decimal place but rounds up or down to the nearest figure. For example, with **double decimal = 0.1234569** the cast to a float with **(float)decimal** produces **0.123457**.

cast.c

1. Begin a new program with a preprocessor instruction to include the standard input/output library functions

```
#include <stdio.h>
```

2. Add a main function that declares and initializes variables of various data types

```
int main()
{
  float num = 5.75 ;
  char letter = 'A' ;
  int zee = 90 ;
  int x = 7 , y = 5 ;
  double decimal = 0.12345678 ;
}
```

3. Next, insert statements to output the cast equivalents of each variable value

```
printf( "Float cast to int: %d \n" , (int)num ) ;
printf( "Char cast to int: %d \n" , (int)letter ) ;
printf( "Int cast to char: %c \n" , (char)zee ) ;
printf( "Float arithmetic: %f \n" , (float)x / (float)y ) ;
printf( "Double cast to float: %f \n" , (float)decimal ) ;
```

4. At the end of the function block, return a zero integer value, as required by the function declaration

```
return 0 ;
```

5. Save the program file, then compile and execute the program to see the resulting equivalent from each cast

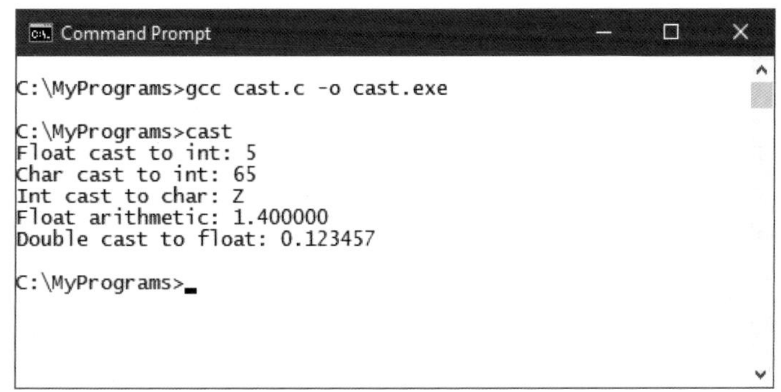

Command Prompt
C:\MyPrograms>gcc cast.c -o cast.exe
C:\MyPrograms>cast
Float cast to int: 5
Char cast to int: 65
Int cast to char: Z
Float arithmetic: 1.400000
Double cast to float: 0.123457
C:\MyPrograms>

Values cast from a **float** to an **int** get truncated but those cast from a **double** to a **float** get rounded.

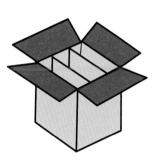

Creating array variables

An array variable can store multiple items of data, unlike a regular variable that can only store a single item of data.

The items of data are stored sequentially in array "elements" that are numbered starting at zero. So, the first array value is stored in array element zero; the second array value is stored in array element one; and so on.

An array variable is declared in a C program in the same way as regular variables but additionally, the size of the array (its number of elements) should be specified in the declaration. This is stated within square brackets following the array name, with this syntax:

data-type array-name **[** ***number-of-elements*** **] ;**

Array elements start numbering at zero, not one.

Optionally, an array can be initialized when it is declared by assigning values to each element as a comma-separated list enclosed by curly brackets (braces). For example, an array of three integers can be created and initialized with **int arr[3] = { 1,2,3 } ;**.

An array element value can be referenced using the array name followed by square brackets containing the element number. For example, **arr[0]** references the value in the first element.

It is acceptable in an array declaration to omit the number between the square brackets if the elements are being initialized in the declaration – the size will be automatically adjusted to accommodate the number of values being assigned to the array.

When creating an array to hold a string, remember to allow space for an element at the end to contain the **\0** null character.

One of the most significant uses of arrays in C programming concerns their ability to store strings of text. Each element in an array of the **char** data type can store a single character. Adding a special **\0** null character escape sequence in the array's final element promotes the array to string status. For example, a string can be created and initialized with **char str[4]={ 'C', 'a', 't', '\0' } ;**.

A character array promoted to string status allows the entire string to be referenced using just the array name, and can be displayed with the **print()** function and the **%s** format specifier – for example, to display a string status array **str** with **printf("%s", str);**.

array.c

1. Begin a new program with a preprocessor instruction to include the standard input/output library functions
```
#include <stdio.h>
```

2. Add a main function that declares an integer array of three elements
```
int main()
{
  int arr[3] ;
}
```

3. Next, insert statements to initialize the integer array elements by individually assigning values to each element
```
arr[0] = 100 ;
arr[1] = 200 ;
arr[2] = 300 ;
```

4. Now, insert a statement to create and initialize a character array to hold a string of text
```
char str[10] = {'C',' ','P','r','o','g','r','a','m','\0' } ;
```

5. Insert statements to output all element values of the integer array and the string from the character array
```
printf( "1st element value: %d \n" , arr[0] ) ;
printf( "2nd element value: %d \n" , arr[1] ) ;
printf( "3rd element value: %d \n" , arr[2] ) ;
printf( "String: %s \n" , str ) ;
```

6. At the end of the function block, return a zero integer value, as required by the function declaration
```
return 0 ;
```

7. Save the program file, then compile and execute the program to see the values stored in the array variables

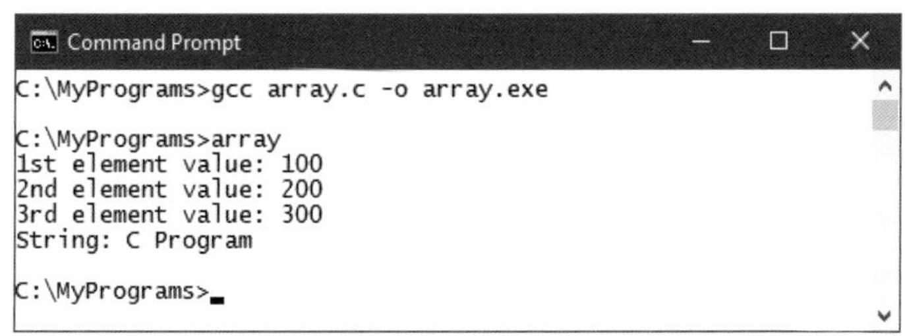

Command Prompt
C:\MyPrograms>gcc array.c -o array.exe
C:\MyPrograms>array
1st element value: 100
2nd element value: 200
3rd element value: 300
String: C Program
C:\MyPrograms>

The creation of an array allocates memory for each element according to the data type – one byte per element for **char** arrays. So, arrays cannot be dynamically resized.

Describing dimensions

The numbering of array elements is more correctly known as the "array index" and, because element numbering starts at zero, is sometimes referred to as a "zero-based index". An array created with a single index is a one-dimensional array in which the elements appear in a single row:

Element content...	A	B	C	D	E
Index numbers...	[0]	[1]	[2]	[3]	[4]

Arrays can also have multiple indices – to represent multiple dimensions. An array created with two indices is a two-dimensional array in which the elements appear in multiple rows:

First index						
First index	[0]	A	B	C	D	E
	[1]	F	G	H	I	J
Second index		[0]	[1]	[2]	[3]	[4]

With multi-dimensional arrays the value contained in each element is referenced by stating the number of each index. For example, with the two-dimensional array above, the element at [1] [2] contains the letter H.

Two-dimensional arrays are useful to store grid-based information, such as XY coordinates. Creating a three-dimensional array, with three indices, would allow XYZ coordinates to be stored:

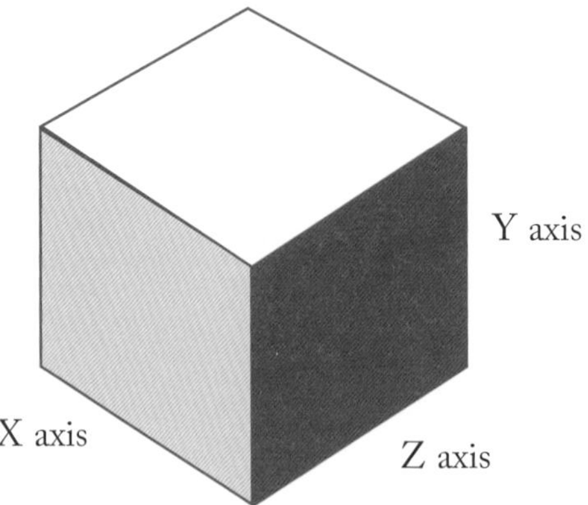

Additional indices allow the creation of arrays with many dimensions, but in reality multi-dimensional arrays of more than three indices are uncommon as they are difficult to envision.

Multi-dimensional arrays with more than two indices can produce hard-to-read source code and may lead to errors.

matrix.c

1. Begin a new program with a preprocessor instruction to include the standard input/output library functions
```
#include <stdio.h>
```

2. Add a main function that declares and initializes a two-dimensional integer array
```
int main()
{
  int matrix[2][3] = { { 'A', 'B', 'C' } , { 1, 2, 3 } } ;
}
```

3. Next, insert statements to display the content of all elements in the first index
```
printf( "Element [0][0] contains %c \n" , matrix[0][0] ) ;
printf( "Element [0][1] contains %c \n" , matrix[0][1] ) ;
printf( "Element [0][2] contains %c \n" , matrix[0][2] ) ;
```

4. Now, insert statements to display the content of all elements in the second index
```
printf( "Element [1][0] contains %d \n" , matrix[1][0] ) ;
printf( "Element [1][1] contains %d \n" , matrix[1][1] ) ;
printf( "Element [1][2] contains %d \n" , matrix[1][2] ) ;
```

5. At the end of the function block, return a zero integer value, as required by the function declaration
```
return 0 ;
```

6. Save the program file, then compile and execute the program to see all the values stored within the two-dimensional array elements

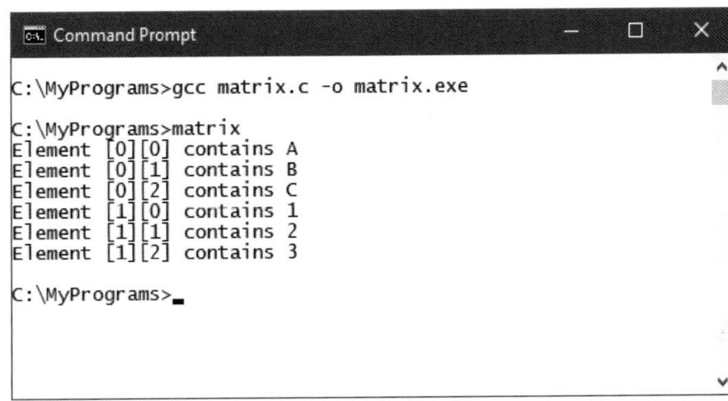

Command Prompt
C:\MyPrograms>gcc matrix.c -o matrix.exe
C:\MyPrograms>matrix
Element [0][0] contains A
Element [0][1] contains B
Element [0][2] contains C
Element [1][0] contains 1
Element [1][1] contains 2
Element [1][2] contains 3
C:\MyPrograms>

Notice here how implicit casting stores the letters' ASCII code values in the integer array but the **%c** format specifier displays them as letters again.

Summary

- A variable is a container in a C program in which a data value can be stored in computer memory.
- Variable names must adhere to the C naming conventions.
- The four basic data types in C are **char, int, float,** and **double.**
- Format specifiers **%d, %f, %c, %s,** and **%p** can be used with the **printf()** function to display variable values of different types.
- User input can be assigned to variables by the **scanf()** function.
- The permissible range of **int** variables can be explicitly qualified using the **short** and **long** keywords.
- Variables that will never hold negative values may be qualified as **unsigned** to extend their positive range.
- The number of memory bytes reserved by any variable can be revealed using the **sizeof** operator.
- Variable scope describes the extent of accessibility to a variable, and may be local or global.
- The **extern** keyword specifies an externally defined variable and the **static** keyword limits accessibility to the same source file.
- Performance of heavily used variables may be improved using the **register** keyword to place the variable in a machine register.
- Variables unsuitable for registers can be marked as **volatile.**
- The compiler may implicitly change data types where that is logical, or they may be changed explicitly by casting.
- Array variables store multiple items of data within individual elements that are sequentially numbered – starting at zero.
- Values in array elements are referenced by the array variable name followed by their element number within square brackets.
- Array variables can have multiple indices to create. multi-dimensional arrays.

3 Setting Constant Values

This chapter demonstrates how to create and utilize constant values and types within C programs.

40 Declaring program constants
42 Enumerating constant values
44 Creating a constant type
46 Defining constants
48 Debugging definitions
50 Summary

Declaring program constants

Where a program is required to use a fixed constant data value that will never change, it should be declared in the same way as a variable, but including the **const** keyword in the declaration. For example, a constant representing the unchanging integer value of one million can be declared and initialized, like this:

```
const int MILLION = 1000000 ;
```

Constant declarations must always initialize the constant object with the data value they will contain. The program can never change the value of a constant from its initial value. This safeguards the constant value from accidental alteration, as the compiler will report an error if the program attempts to subsequently alter the initial value.

Constant names are subject to the same naming conventions as variable names (described on page 20) but it is traditional to use uppercase characters for constant names – to easily distinguish them from variable names when reading the source code.

The **const** keyword can also be used in an array declaration if all its initial element values are never to be changed by the program.

constant.c

1. Begin a new program with a preprocessor instruction to include the standard input/output library functions

```
#include <stdio.h>
```

2. Add a main function that declares a constant value approximating the mathematical value of Pi

```
int main()
{
  const float PI = 3.141593 ;
}
```

3. Next, in the main function block, insert statements declaring four variables

```
float diameter ;
float radius ;
float circ ;
float area ;
```

4. Now, insert statements requesting user input to be assigned to a variable
   printf("Enter the diameter of a circle in millimeters: ") ;
   scanf("%f" , &diameter) ;

5. Next, add statements to calculate values for the other three variables using the constant value and user input
   circ = PI * diameter ;
   radius = diameter / 2 ;
   area = PI * (radius * radius) ;

6. Now, insert statements to output the calculated values formatted to two decimal places
   printf("\n\tCircumference is %.2f mm" , circ) ;
   printf("\n\tAnd the area is %.2f sq.mm\n" , area) ;

7. At the end of the main function block, return a zero integer value, as required by the function declaration
   return 0 ;

8. Save the program file, then compile and execute the program, entering data when requested, to see the calculated output

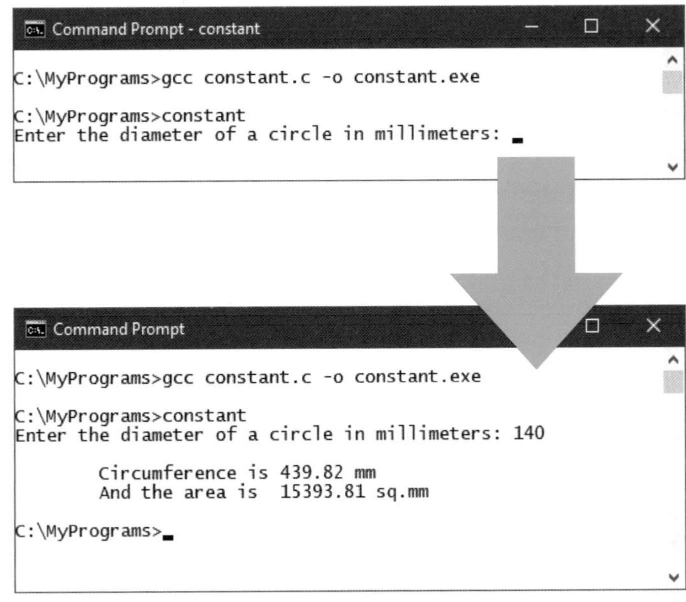

Here the * asterisk character is the arithmetical multiplication operator, and the / forward slash character is the division operator. Arithmetical operators are demonstrated fully in the next chapter.

Remember that the **&** addressof operator must precede the variable name in **scanf()** to assign input to the variable.

Enumerating constant values

The **enum** keyword provides a handy way to create a sequence of integer constants in a concise manner. Optionally, the declaration can include a name for the sequence after the **enum** keyword. The constant names follow as a comma-separated list within braces.

Each of the constants will, by default, have a value one greater than that of the constant it follows in the list. Unless specified, the first constant will have a value of zero; the next a value of 1; and so on.

For example, named weekday constants can be given a sequence of integer values starting at zero with **enum{MON,TUE.WED.THU,FRI};** – in this case, the constant **WED** has an integer value of 2.

The constants can be assigned any individual integer value in the declaration but the next constant in the list will always increment the preceding value by one, unless it too is assigned a value. For example, to begin the sequence at 1 instead of zero, assign 1 to the first constant with **enum{MON=1,TUE,WED,THU,FRI};** – in this case, the constant **WED** has an integer value of 3.

The list of enumerated constants is also known as an "enumeration set" and may contain duplicate constant values. For example, the value zero could be assigned to constants named **NIL** and **NONE**.

In the following example, the enumeration set represents the points value of balls in the game of snooker, and includes an optional name, which appears in uppercase as it too is constant.

enum.c

1. Begin a new program with a preprocessor instruction to include the standard input/output library functions
```
#include <stdio.h>
```

2. Add a main function that declares and initializes an enumerated set of constants starting at 1
```
int main()
{
  enum SNOOKER
  { RED=1,YELLOW, GREEN, BROWN, BLUE, PINK, BLACK } ;
}
```

3. Next, in the main function block, declare an integer variable to store the sum of some constant values
```
int total ;
```

4. Now, insert statements to display the value of some of the enumerated constants

```
printf( "\nI potted a red worth %d\n" , RED ) ;
printf( "Then a black worth %d\n" , BLACK ) ;
printf( "Followed by another red worth %d\n" , RED ) ;
printf( "And finally a blue worth %d\n" , BLUE ) ;
```

5. Next, add a statement to calculate the sum total of the constant values displayed by the previous step

```
total = RED + BLACK + RED + BLUE ;
```

6. Now, add a statement to output the calculated total of the displayed values

```
printf( "\nAltogether I scored %d\n" , total ) ;
```

7. At the end of the main function block, return a zero integer value, as required by the function declaration

```
return 0 ;
```

8. Save the program file, then compile and execute the program to see the enumerated constant values and the calculated total in the output

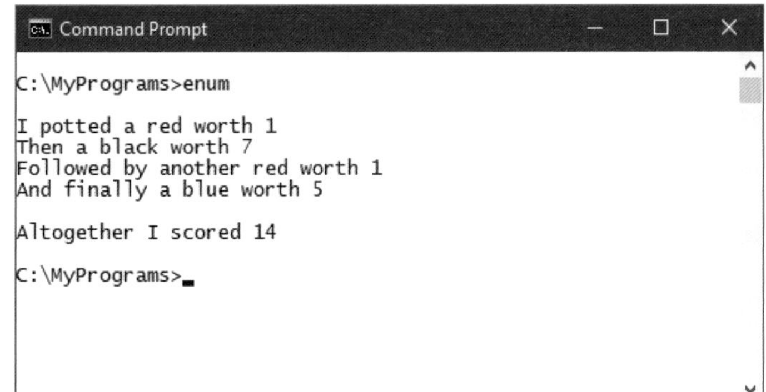
Command Prompt
C:\MyPrograms>enum
I potted a red worth 1
Then a black worth 7
Followed by another red worth 1
And finally a blue worth 5
Altogether I scored 14
C:\MyPrograms>_

Beware

Assigning a value of 1 to the **BLUE** constant in this example restarts the incrementing process – making the **PINK** constant 2 and the **BLACK** constant 3.

Don't forget

The enum type name (in this case, **SNOOKER**) is optional – so may be omitted in this example.

Creating a constant type

Once an enumerated sequence is declared it can be considered to be like a new data type in its own right, with properties of its specified constant names and their associated values.

Variables of this **enum** data type can be declared in the same way that variables are declared of other data types – using this syntax:

data-type variable-name ;

The example on pages 42-43 created an enumerated sequence named **SNOOKER**, which can be regarded as a data type of **enum SNOOKER**. So a variable named "pair" of that data type can be created with the declaration **enum SNOOKER pair** ; and can store values of the enumeration set defined by that type.

To explicitly assign an integer value to a variable of an enumerated data type, the C standard recommends that a cast be used to convert the **int** data type to the **enum** data type, like this:

```
pair = ( enum SNOOKER ) 7 ;
```

In practice this is not needed though, as enumerated values are always integers so are equivalent to the **int** data type.

An **enum** declaration can optionally also create a variable by specifying a variable name after the final brace. For example, the declaration **enum BOOLEAN { FALSE , TRUE } flag** ; defines an **enum** data type and creates a variable named "flag" of that type.

Custom data types can be defined using the **typedef** keyword and this syntax:

typedef ***definition type-name*** ;

Declaration of custom data types can help make the program code more concise. For example, where a program uses a number of **unsigned short int** variables it would be useful to first create a custom data type with those modifiers, using this declaration:

```
typedef unsigned short int USINT ;
```

Each **unsigned short int** variable declaration can then simply use the custom data type name **USINT** in place of **unsigned short int**.

Although not essential, using the recommended cast to explicitly assign values to an enumerated type variable serves as a reminder of its type.

constype.c

1. Begin a new program with a preprocessor instruction to include the standard input/output library functions
```
#include <stdio.h>
```

2. Add a main function that declares and initializes an enumerated set of constants starting at 1
```
int main()
{
  enum SNOOKER
  { RED=1,YELLOW, GREEN, BROWN, BLUE, PINK, BLACK } ;
}
```

3. Next, in the main function block, declare and initialize a variable of the defined enum type, then display its value
```
enum SNOOKER pair = RED + BLACK ;
printf( "Pair value: %d \n" , pair ) ;
```

4. Now, add a statement to create a custom data type
```
typedef unsigned short int USINT ;
```

5. Then, declare and initialize a variable of the custom data type and display its value
```
USINT num = 16 ;
printf( "Unsigned short int value: %d \n" , num ) ;
```

6. At the end of the main function block, return a zero integer value, as required by the function declaration
```
return 0 ;
```

7. Save the program file, then compile and execute the program to see the value assigned to the enumerated type variable and to the custom data type

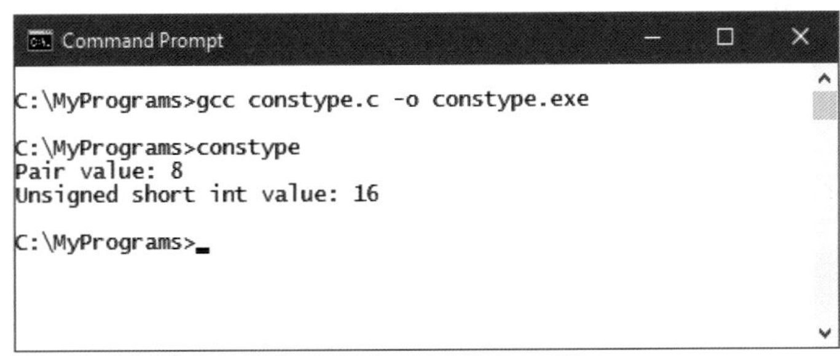

Command Prompt
C:\MyPrograms>gcc constype.c -o constype.exe
C:\MyPrograms>constype
Pair value: 8
Unsigned short int value: 16
C:\MyPrograms>

Custom data types must be defined in the program before variables of that type can be created.

Defining constants

The preprocessor **#define** directive can be used to specify constant text values that can be used in a program with this syntax:

#define *CONSTANT-NAME "text-string"*

Like the **#include** directive, these should appear at the very start of the program code. Any occurrences of the specified constant name in the program code will be substituted for the associated text string by the preprocessor before compilation.

A conditional preprocessor **#ifdef** directive can also be used to evaluate whether a definition currently exists. Depending on the result of the evaluation it may be followed by a **#define** directive to specify a constant text value. This preprocessor routine is known as a "macro" and each macro must end with an **#endif** directive.

Usefully, a preprocessor macro can examine compiler-defined constants to determine the host operating system. These will vary from machine to machine, but on the Windows platform there will typically be a constant named **_WIN32**, and on the Linux platform there will typically be a **linux** constant. An **#ifdef** preprocessor directive can apply an appropriate text string to identify the host platform.

define.c

1. Begin a new program with a preprocessor instruction to include the standard input/output library functions
```
#include <stdio.h>
```

2. Add three further preprocessor directives that specify text strings for substitution in the source code
```
#define LINE "____________________"
#define TITLE "C Programming in easy steps"
#define AUTHOR "Mike McGrath"
```

3. Next, add a conditional macro that specifies a text string to identify the Windows host platform
```
#ifdef _WIN32
#define SYSTEM "Windows"
#endif
```

4. Now, add a conditional macro that specifies a text string to identify the Linux host platform

```
#ifdef linux
#define SYSTEM "Linux"
#endif
```

5. Next, add a main function that outputs the text string values substituted by the preprocessor

```
int main()
{
  printf( "\n \t %s \n \t %s \n" , LINE , TITLE ) ;
  printf( "\t by %s \n \t %s \n" , AUTHOR , LINE ) ;
  printf( "\n Operating System: %s \n" , SYSTEM ) ;
}
```

6. At the end of the main function block, return a zero integer value, as required by the function declaration

```
return 0 ;
```

7. Save the program file, then compile and execute the program to see the string constants output

```
Command Prompt

C:\MyPrograms>gcc define.c -o define.exe

C:\MyPrograms>define

        ______________________________
        C Programming in easy steps
        by Mike McGrath
        ______________________________

 Operating System: Windows

C:\MyPrograms>_
```

The **LINE** string in this example is just a series of underscore characters.

Try issuing the command **cpp -dM define.c** to see all the defined constants.

Debugging definitions

Alternatives can be offered with **#if**, **#else** and **#elif** (else if) preprocessor directives. These allow conditional branching to execute sections of code according to the result of an evaluation.

A constant initially defined by a preprocessor **#define** directive can be subsequently undefined with an **#undef** directive. An evaluation may also be made to consider whether a constant is undefined with an **#ifndef** (if not defined) preprocessor directive.

All evaluations can be made in a function block, mixed with regular C statements, and may be nested one within another. Macros of this kind are particularly useful for debugging source code, as whole sections of the code can be easily hidden or revealed, simply by changing the status of a **DEBUG** macro.

debug.c

1. Begin a new program with a preprocessor instruction to include the standard input/output library functions

```
#include <stdio.h>
```

2. Add a further preprocessor directive to establish a macro

```
#define DEBUG 1
```

3. Next, add a main function containing preprocessor directives to evaluate and report the macro status

```
#if DEBUG == 1
  printf( "Debug status is 1 \n" );
#elif DEBUG == 2
  printf( "Debug status is 2 \n" ) ;
#else
  #ifdef DEBUG
    printf( "Debug is defined! \n" ) ;
  #endif
  #ifndef DEBUG
    printf( "Debug is not defined! \n" ) ;
  #endif
#endif
```

4. At the end of the main function block, return a zero integer value, as required by the function declaration

```
return 0 ;
```

The == equality operator used in this example means "is equal to".

5. Save the program file, then compile and execute the program to see the macro status reported

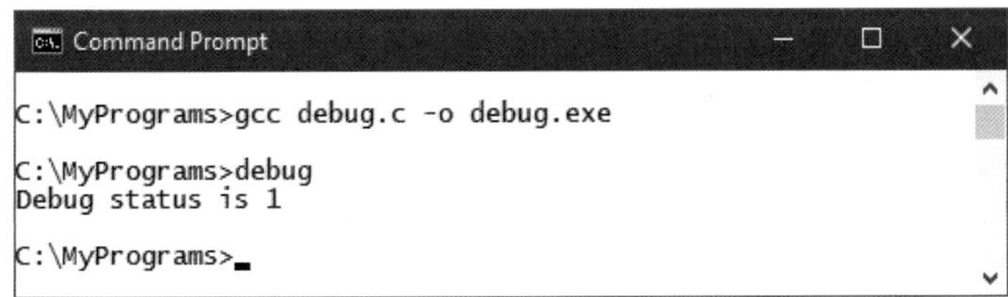
Command Prompt
C:\MyPrograms>gcc debug.c -o debug.exe
C:\MyPrograms>debug
Debug status is 1
C:\MyPrograms>_

6. Modify the macro value then save, recompile, and execute the program again to see the new macro status reported
   #define DEBUG 2

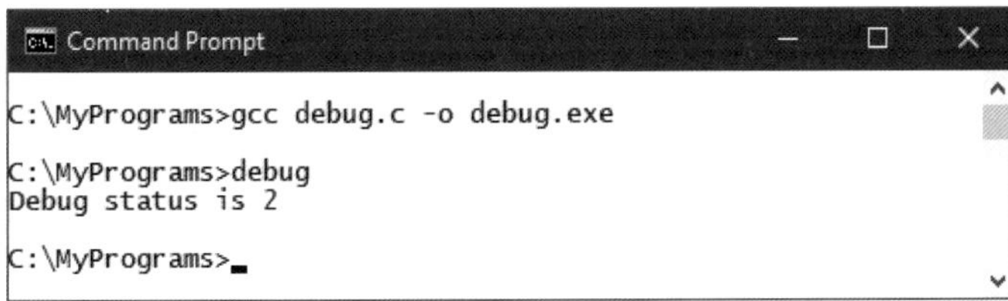
Command Prompt
C:\MyPrograms>gcc debug.c -o debug.exe
C:\MyPrograms>debug
Debug status is 2
C:\MyPrograms>_

7. Modify the macro value once more then save, recompile, and execute the program again to see the change
   #define DEBUG 3

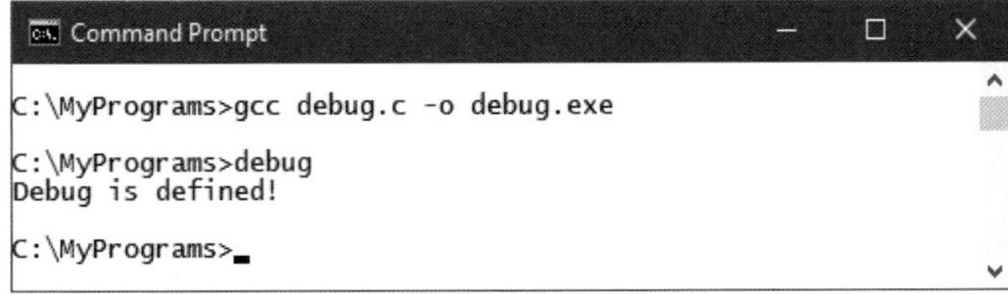
Command Prompt
C:\MyPrograms>gcc debug.c -o debug.exe
C:\MyPrograms>debug
Debug is defined!
C:\MyPrograms>_

Don't forget

Every preprocessor conditional test must end with an **#endif** directive.

8. Insert another preprocessor directive at the start of the function block then save, recompile, and execute the program again to see the macro status reported
   #undef DEBUG

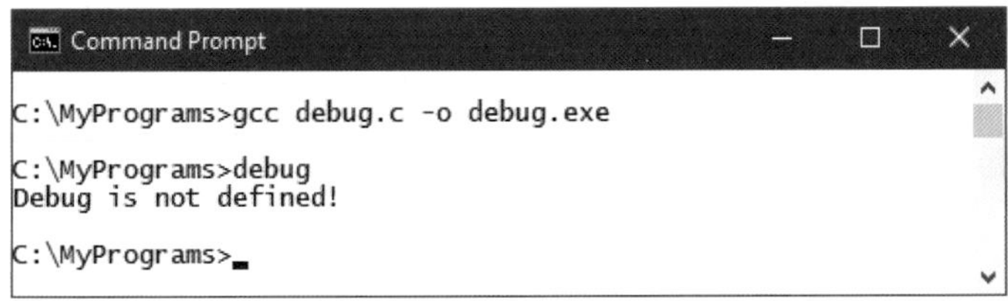
Command Prompt
C:\MyPrograms>gcc debug.c -o debug.exe
C:\MyPrograms>debug
Debug is not defined!
C:\MyPrograms>_

Summary

- A fixed data value that will never change should be stored as a constant, declared with the **const** keyword.
- When declaring a constant the declaration must always initialize the constant with its fixed data value.
- The **enum** keyword creates a sequentially numbered series of integer constants that, by default, start at zero.
- Any constant in an enumerated series can be explicitly assigned an integer value, which subsequent constants in that series will increment.
- An enumerated series of constants can be regarded as a new data type, from which variables can be created to store values of the enumeration set defined by that type.
- A custom data type can be defined using the **typedef** keyword, then variables of that type can be created using the same syntax as that used to declare regular variables.
- A preprocessor **#define** directive can be used to specify a constant text value to be substituted before compilation.
- The conditional preprocessor **#ifdef** directive evaluates whether a definition currently exists.
- A macro is a preprocessor routine that must end with an **#endif** directive.
- Compiler-defined constants, such as **_WIN32** and **linux**, can determine the host operating system.
- Macro alternatives can be offered with **#if**, **#else**, and **#elif** preprocessor directives.
- Constant macro definitions can be undefined with the **#undef** directive, and evaluated as undefined with the **#ifndef** directive.
- Macros can be useful to aid debugging of source code by easily hiding or revealing sections of code.

4 Performing Operations

This chapter demonstrates how the C operators are used to manipulate data within a C program.

52 Doing arithmetic
54 Assigning values
56 Comparing values
58 Assessing logic
60 Examining conditions
62 Measuring size
64 Comparing bit values
66 Flagging bits
68 Understanding precedence
70 Summary

Doing arithmetic

The arithmetic operators commonly used in C programs are listed in the table below, together with the operation they perform:

Operator:	Operation:
+	Addition
-	Subtraction
*	Multiplication
/	Division
%	Modulus
++	Increment
--	Decrement

Operators for addition, subtraction, multiplication, and division act as you would expect. Care must be taken, however, to bracket expressions for clarity where more than one operator is used:

```
a = b * c - d % e / f ;            /* This is unclear. */

a = ( b * c ) - ( ( d % e ) / f ) ;  /* This is clearer. */
```

The **%** modulus operator divides the first given number by the second given number and returns the remainder of the operation. This is useful to determine if a number has an odd or even value.

The ++ increment operator and -- decrement operator alter the given number by one and return the resulting new value. These are most often used to count iterations in a loop. The increment operator increases the value by one and the decrement operator decreases the value by one.

The increment and decrement operators can be placed before or after an operand to different effect. If placed before the operand (prefix) its value is changed immediately; if placed after the operand (postfix) its value is first noted then changed later.

The numbers used along with operators to form expressions are known as "operands" – in the expression **2 + 3** the numbers **2** and **3** are the operands.

arithmetic.c

1. Begin a new program with a preprocessor instruction to include the standard input/output library functions

```
#include <stdio.h>
```

2. Add a main function that declares and initializes several integer variables

```
int main()
{
  int a = 4 , b = 8 , c = 1 , d = 1 ;
}
```

3. Next, in the main function block, output the result of arithmetical operations performed on the variable values

```
printf( "Addition: %d \n" , a + b ) ;
printf( "Subtraction: %d \n" , b - a ) ;
printf( "Multiplication: %d \n" , a * b ) ;
printf( "Division: %d \n" , b / a ) ;
printf( "Modulus: %d \n" , a % b ) ;
```

4. Now, in the main function block, output the result of both postfix and prefix increment operations

```
printf( "Postfix increment: %d \n" , c++ ) ;
printf( "Postfix now: %d \n" , c ) ;
printf( "Prefix increment: %d \n" , ++d ) ;
printf( "Prefix now: %d \n" , d ) ;
```

5. At the end of the main function block, return a zero integer value, as required by the function declaration

```
return 0 ;
```

6. Save the program file, then compile and execute the program to see the results of the arithmetical operations

```
Command Prompt
C:\MyPrograms>gcc arithmetic.c -o arithmetic.exe

C:\MyPrograms>arithmetic
Addition: 12
Subtraction: 4
Multiplication: 32
Division: 2
Modulus: 4
Postfix increment: 1
Postfix now: 2
Prefix increment: 2
Prefix now: 2

C:\MyPrograms>
```

Notice that the variable value is immediately increased only with the prefix increment operator – with the postfix operator it is incremented the next time it is referenced.

Assigning values

The operators that are used in C programs to assign values are listed in the table below. All except the simple = assign operator are a shorthand form of a longer expression, so each equivalent is given for clarity.

Operator:	Example:	Equivalent:
=	a = b	a = b
+=	a += b	a = (a + b)
-=	a -= b	a = (a - b)
*=	a *= b	a = (a * b)
/=	a /= b	a = (a / b)
%=	a %= b	a = (a % b)

The == equality operator compares operand values. This is described on page 56.

It is important to regard the = operator to mean "assign" rather than "equals" to avoid confusion with the == equality operator.

In the example above, the variable named **a** is assigned the value that is contained in the variable named **b** – so that becomes the new value stored in the **a** variable.

The **+=** operator is useful to add a value onto an existing value that is stored in the **a** variable. In the table example, the **+=** operator first adds the value stored in the variable **a** to the value stored in the variable **b**. It then assigns the result to become the new value stored in the **a** variable.

All the other operators in the table work in the same way by making the arithmetical operation between the two values first, then assigning the result to the first variable to become its new stored value.

With the **%=** operator, the first operand **a** is divided by the second operand **b**, then the remainder of the operation is assigned to the **a** variable.

assign.c

1. Begin a new program with a preprocessor instruction to include the standard input/output library functions

```
#include <stdio.h>
```

2. Add a main function that declares two integer variables

```
int main()
{
  int a , b ;
}
```

3. Next, in the main function block, output the result of assignment operations performed on the variables

```
printf( "Assigned: \n" ) ;
printf( "\tVariable a = %d \n" , a = 8 ) ;
printf( "\tVariable b = %d \n" , b = 4 ) ;
printf( "Added & assigned: \n" ) ;
printf( "\tVariable a+=b (8+=4) a= %d \n", a += b ) ;
printf( "Subtracted & assigned: \n" ) ;
printf( "\tVariable a-=b (12-=4) a= %d \n", a -= b ) ;
printf( "Multiplied & assigned: \n" ) ;
printf( "\tVariable a*=b (8*=4) a= %d \n", a *= b ) ;
printf( "Divided & assigned: \n" ) ;
printf( "\tVariable a/=b (32/=4) a= %d \n", a /= b ) ;
printf( "Modulated & assigned: \n" ) ;
printf( "\tVariable a%%=b (8%%=4) a= %d \n", a %= b ) ;
```

4. At the end of the main function block, return a zero integer value, as required by the function declaration

```
return 0 ;
```

5. Save the program file, then compile and execute the program to see the results of the assignment operations

```
Command Prompt
C:\MyPrograms>assign
Assigned:
        Variable a = 8
        Variable b = 4
Added & assigned:
        Variable a+=b (8+=4) a= 12
Subtracted & assigned:
        Variable a-=b (12-=4) a= 8
Multiplied & assigned:
        Variable a*=b (8*=4) a= 32
Divided & assigned:
        Variable a/=b (32/=4) a= 8
Modulated & assigned:
        Variable a%=b (8%=4) a= 0

C:\MyPrograms>_
```

Notice that **%%** must be used in order to display the **%** character with the **printf()** function.

Comparing values

The operators that are commonly used in C programming to compare two numerical values are listed in the table below:

Operator:	Comparative test:
==	Equality
!=	Inequality
>	Greater than
<	Less than
>=	Greater than or equal to
<=	Less than or equal to

The == equality operator compares two operands and will return **1** (true) if both are equal in value, otherwise it will return **0** (false). If both are the same number they are equal, or if both are characters their ASCII code value is compared numerically.

Conversely, the **!=** inequality operator returns **1** (true) if the two operands are not equal, using the same rules as the == equality operator; otherwise it returns **0** (false).

Equality and inequality operators are useful in testing the state of two variables to perform conditional branching in a program.

The **>** "greater than" operator compares two operands and will return **1** (true) if the first is greater in value than the second, or it will return **0** (false) if it is equal or less in value. The **>** "greater than" operator is frequently used to test the value of a countdown value in a loop.

The **<** "less than" operator makes the same comparison but returns **1** (true) if the first operand is less in value than the second, otherwise it returns **0** (false).

Adding the = operator after a **>** "greater than" or **<** "less than" operator makes it also return **1** (true) when the two operands are exactly equal in value.

Further information on ASCII code values can be found in the Reference section on pages 162-163.

comparison.c

1. Begin a new program with a preprocessor instruction to include the standard input/output library functions

```
#include <stdio.h>
```

2. Add a main function that declares and initializes three integer variables and two character variables

```
int main()
{
  int zero = 0 , nil = 0 , one = 1 ;
  char upr = 'A' , lwr = 'a' ;
}
```

3. Next, in the main function block, output the result of comparison operations performed on the variables

```
printf( "Equality (0==0): %d \n" , zero == nil ) ;
printf( "Equality (0==1): %d \n" , zero == one ) ;
printf( "Equality (A==a): %d \n" , upr == lwr ) ;
printf( "Inequality (A!=a): %d \n" , upr != lwr ) ;
printf( "Greater than (1>0): %d \n" , one > nil ) ;
printf( "Less than (1<0): %d \n" , one < nil ) ;
printf( "Greater or equal (0>=0): %d \n" , zero >= nil ) ;
printf( "Less or equal (1<=0): %d \n" , one <= nil ) ;
```

4. At the end of the main function block, return a zero integer value, as required by the function declaration

```
return 0 ;
```

5. Save the program file, then compile and execute the program to see the results of the comparison operations

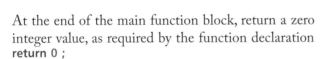

```
Command Prompt

C:\MyPrograms>gcc comparison.c -o comparison.exe

C:\MyPrograms>comparison
Equality (0==0): 1
Equality (0==1): 0
Equality (A==a): 0
Inequality (A!=a): 1
Greater than (1>0): 1
Less than (1<0): 0
Greater or equal (0>=0): 1
Less or equal (1<=0): 0

C:\MyPrograms>_
```

Numerically, **1** represents a true result and **0** represents a false result.

The ASCII code value for uppercase 'A' is 65 and for lowercase 'a' it's 97 – so their comparison here returns **0** (false).

Assessing logic

The logical operators most commonly used in C programming are listed in the table below:

Operator:	Operation:
&&	Logical AND
||	Logical OR
!	Logical NOT

The logical operators are used with operands that have the Boolean values of true or false, or an expression that can convert to true or false.

The logical **&&** AND operator will evaluate two operands and return true only if both operands are themselves true. Otherwise, the **&&** AND operator will return false.

This is used in conditional branching, where the direction of a C program is determined by testing two conditions. If both conditions are satisfied, the program will go in a certain direction, otherwise it will take a different direction.

Unlike the **&&** AND operator that needs both operands to be true, the **||** OR operator will evaluate two operands and return true if either one of the operands is itself true. If neither operand is true then the **||** OR operator will return false. This is useful in C programming to perform a certain action if either one of two test conditions has been met.

The third logical **!** NOT operator is a "unary" operator – that is used before a single operand. It returns the inverse value of the given operand, so if the variable **var** is a true value then **!var** would return a false value. The **!** NOT operator is useful in C programming to toggle the value of a variable in successive loop iterations with a statement like **var = !var**. This ensures that on each pass the value is reversed, like flicking a light switch on and off.

In C programming, a zero represents the Boolean false value; and any non-zero value, such as **1**, represents the Boolean true value.

The term "Boolean" refers to a system of logical thought developed by the English mathematician George Boole (1815-1864).

logic.c

1. Begin a new program with a preprocessor instruction to include the standard input/output library functions

```
#include <stdio.h>
```

2. Add a main function that declares and initializes two integer variables

```
int main()
{
  int yes = 1 , no = 0 ;
}
```

3. Next, in the main function block, output the result of logic operations performed on the variables

```
printf( "AND (no&&no): %d \n" , no && no ) ;
printf( "AND (yes&&no): %d \n" , yes && no ) ;
printf( "AND (yes&&yes): %d \n" , yes && yes ) ;
printf( "OR (no||no): %d \n" , no || no ) ;
printf( "OR (yes||no): %d \n" , yes || no ) ;
printf( "OR (yes||yes): %d \n" , yes || yes ) ;
printf( "NOT (yes !yes): %d %d\n" , yes , !yes ) ;
printf( "NOT (no !no): %d %d\n" , no , !no ) ;
```

4. At the end of the main function block, return a zero integer value, as required by the function declaration

```
return 0 ;
```

5. Save the program file, then compile and execute the program to see the results of the logic operations

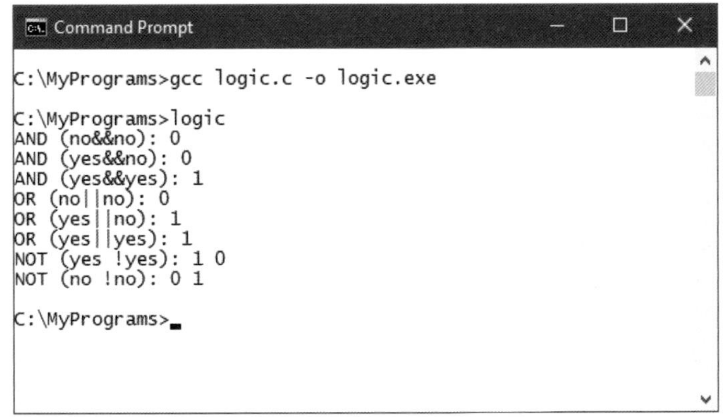

Command Prompt
C:\MyPrograms>gcc logic.c -o logic.exe
C:\MyPrograms>logic
AND (no&&no): 0
AND (yes&&no): 0
AND (yes&&yes): 1
OR (no||no): 0
OR (yes||no): 1
OR (yes||yes): 1
NOT (yes !yes): 1 0
NOT (no !no): 0 1
C:\MyPrograms>

Notice that **0 && 0** returns **0** (false) – demonstrating the anecdote "two wrongs don't make a right".

Examining conditions

Possibly the C programmer's favorite test operator is the **?:** conditional operator, also known as the "ternary" operator. This operator first evaluates an expression for a true or false Boolean value, then executes one of two given statements depending on the result of the evaluation.

The conditional operator has this syntax:

(*test-expression*) ? *if-true-do-this* : *if-false-do-this* ;

This operator could, for example, be used to evaluate whether a given number is odd or even by examining if there is any remainder after dividing the number by two, then output an appropriate string, like this:

```
( 7 % 2 != 0 ) ? printf( "Odd Number" ) : printf( "Even Number" ) ;
```

In this case, dividing seven by two does not leave a zero remainder – so the expression evaluates as true; therefore the first statement is executed, correctly describing the number as an odd value.

The conditional operator is also useful to ensure correct grammar in output regarding singular and plural items, thus avoiding awkward phrases like "There is 5". The evaluation can simply be made within the **printf()** statement to use the appropriate version:

```
printf( "There %s %d" , ( num == 1 ) ? "is" : "are" , num ) ;
```

In this case, when it's true that the **num** variable has a value of one, the "is" version will be used, otherwise the "are" version will be used.

Although the conditional operator is quick and easy to use it can reduce code readability.

The conditional operator can also be used to assign an appropriate value to a variable depending on the result of an evaluation. Used in this way its syntax looks like this:

***variable* = (*test-expression*) ? *if-true-assign-this* : *if-false-assign-this* ;**

This operator could, for example, be used to evaluate whether one given number is greater than another then assign the greater number to a variable, like this:

```
int num , a = 5 , b = 2 ;
num = ( a > b ) ? a : b ;
```

In this case, the value of variable **a** is greater than that of variable **b**, so the **num** variable is assigned the greater value of **5**.

conditional.c

1. Begin a new program with a preprocessor instruction to include the standard input/output library functions

```
#include <stdio.h>
```

2. Add a main function that declares and initializes a single integer variable

```
int main()
{
  int num = 7 ;
}
```

3. Next, in the main function block, insert a conditional statement to output the variable value's parity

```
( num % 2 != 0 ) ?
printf("%d is odd\n", num) :  printf("%d is even\n", num) ;
```

4. Now, insert conditional statements to output a phrase using correct grammar for plurals

```
printf( "There %s " , ( num == 1 ) ? "is" : "are" ) ;
printf( "%d %s\n", num, (num==1) ? "apple" : "apples" ) ;
```

5. Decrease the variable value then insert conditional statements to output a phrase correct for singularity

```
num=1;
printf( "There %s " , (num == 1) ? "is" : "are" ) ;
printf( "%d %s\n", num, (num==1) ? "apple" : "apples" ) ;
```

6. At the end of the main function block, return a zero integer value, as required by the function declaration

```
return 0 ;
```

7. Save the program file, then compile and execute the program to see the results of the conditional operations

The conditional operator is best used for terse statements that offer just two simple alternatives to implement.

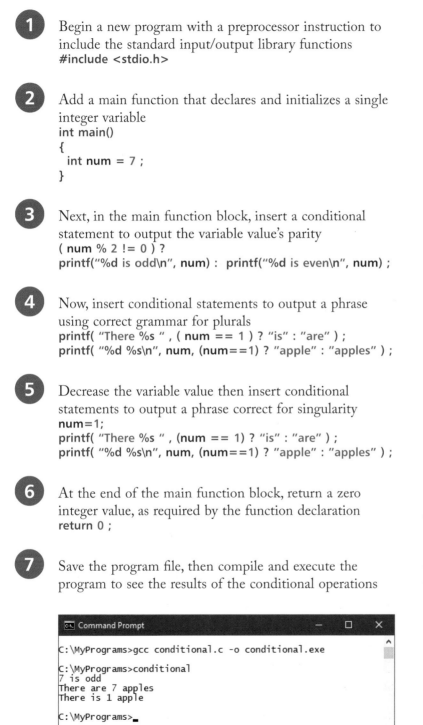

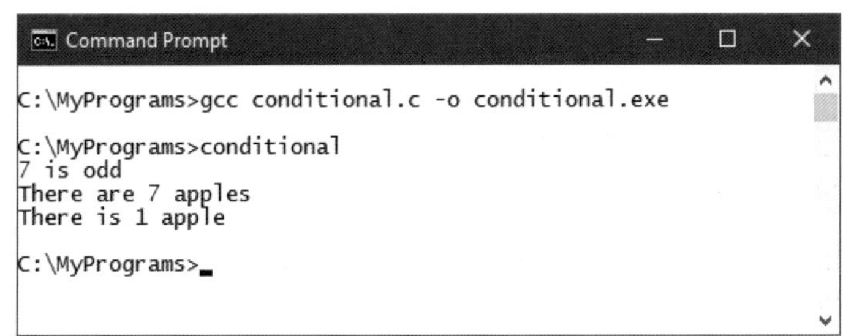

Command Prompt
C:\MyPrograms>gcc conditional.c -o conditional.exe
C:\MyPrograms>conditional
7 is odd
There are 7 apples
There is 1 apple
C:\MyPrograms>

Measuring size

In C programming, the **sizeof** operator returns an integer value, which is the number of bytes needed to store the content of its operand in memory.

Where the operand supplied to the **sizeof** operator is a data type name, such as **int**, the operand must be enclosed within parentheses – as with the examples listed earlier on page 27.

Alternatively, where the supplied operand is a data object name, such as a variable name, the parentheses may optionally be omitted. In practice, many programmers will always enclose the **sizeof** operator's operand within parentheses to avoid having to remember this distinction.

The basic storage unit in C is defined by the **char** data type that stores a single character in a single byte of memory. This means that **sizeof(char)** will return **1** (1 byte).

Typically, the **int** and **float** data types will each allocate 4 bytes of machine memory, whereas the **double** data type will typically allocate 8 bytes of machine memory to accommodate its range of possible values. These sizes are not defined by the standards, however, but are implementation-defined so may vary. It is therefore good practice to use the **sizeof** operator to measure the actual memory allocation rather than assume these typical sizes will be allocated.

The memory space allocated for array variables will simply be the number of bytes allocated for that data type multiplied by the number of elements in that array. So, for example, the expression **sizeof(int[3])** will typically return **12** (3 x 4 bytes).

It is especially important to use the **sizeof** operator to accurately discover the amount of memory allocated for user-defined structures that have members of different data types, as "padding" is often automatically added. This means that total memory allocation may exceed the sum allocated to each member. It might seem reasonable to expect that a structure comprising member variables **int score** and **char grade** will be allocated total memory of 5 bytes (4+1), but the total allocation will typically be 8 bytes. This is because computer systems like to read and write data in "word"-sized chunks of 4 bytes each. So, padding gets added to make the memory allocation a multiple of four.

Hot tip

Always enclose an operand supplied to the **sizeof** operator within parentheses for code consistency.

size.c

1. Begin a new program with a preprocessor instruction to include the standard input/output library functions
```
#include <stdio.h>
```

2. Add a main function that declares and initializes a single integer variable
```
int main()
{
  int num = 1234567890 ;
}
```

3. Next, in the main function block, insert statements to reveal the memory allocated to the **int** data type (in this implementation) by type name and object name
```
printf( "Size of int data type is %d bytes\n" , sizeof (int) ) ;
printf( "Size of int variable is %d bytes\n" , sizeof (num) ) ;
```

4. Now, insert a statement to reveal that an array allocates the same memory for each one of its elements
```
printf( "Size of an int array is %d bytes\n", sizeof (int[3]) ) ;
```

5. Define a structure comprising one char variable and one int variable then reveal its total memory allocation – including any padding
```
struct { int score ; char grade ; } result ;
printf("Size of a structure is %d bytes\n" , sizeof (result) ) ;
```

6. At the end of the main function block, return a zero integer value, as required by the function declaration
```
return 0 ;
```

7. Save the program file, then compile and execute the program to see output from the **sizeof** operations

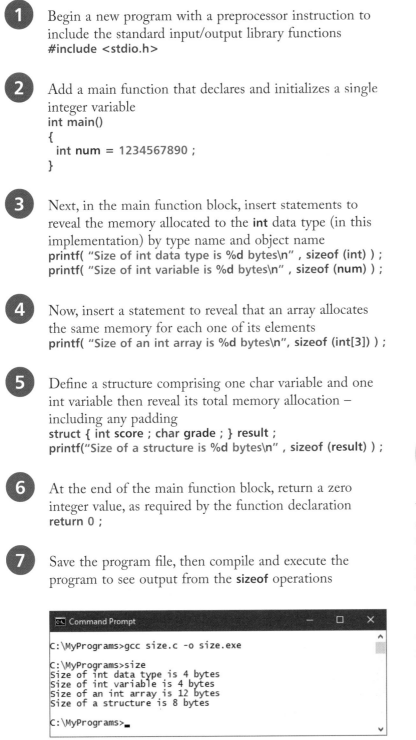

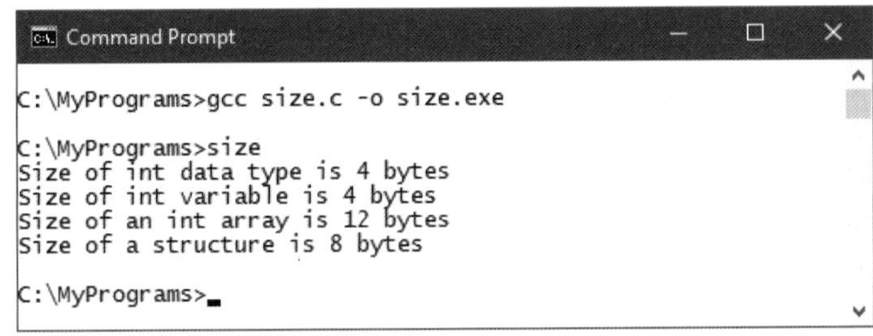
Command Prompt
C:\MyPrograms>gcc size.c -o size.exe
C:\MyPrograms>size
Size of int data type is 4 bytes
Size of int variable is 4 bytes
Size of an int array is 12 bytes
Size of a structure is 8 bytes
C:\MyPrograms>

Don't forget

This example includes code for a **struct** object, which is a list of different variables. Structures are demonstrated in Chapter 9 but a **struct** is included here to demonstrate how the **sizeof** operator can measure its memory size.

Comparing bit values

A byte comprises 8 bits that can each contain a **1** or a **0** to store a binary number representing decimal values from 0 to 255. Each bit contributes a decimal component only when that bit contains a **1**. Components are designated right-to-left from the "Least Significant Bit" (LSB) to the "Most Significant Bit" (MSB). The binary number in the bit pattern below represents decimal 50.

Many C programmers never use bitwise operators but it is useful to understand what they are and how they may be used.

Bit No.	8 MSB	7	6	5	4	3	2	1 LSB
Decimal	128	64	32	16	8	4	2	1
Binary	0	0	1	1	0	0	1	0

Although the **char** data type is the basic 1-byte storage unit in C programming, as described on page 62, it is possible to manipulate individual parts of a byte using "bitwise" operators.

Each half of a byte is known as a "nibble" (4 bits). The binary numbers in the examples in the table describe values stored in a nibble.

Operator:	Name:	Binary number operation:
|	OR	Return a **1** in each bit where either of two compared bits is a **1** Example: **1010 | 0101 = 1111**
&	AND	Return a **1** in each bit where both of two compared bits is a **1** Example: **1010 & 1100 = 1000**
~	NOT	Return a **1** in each bit where the bit is not **1**, and return **0** where the bit is **1** Example: **~ 1010 = 0101**
^	XOR	Return a **1** in each bit where only one of two compared bits is a **1** Example: **1010 ^ 0100 = 1110**
<<	Shift left	Move each bit that is a **1** a specified number of bits to the left Example: **0010 << 2 = 1000**
>>	Shift right	Move each bit that is a **1** a specified number of bits to the right Example: **1000 >> 2 = 0010**

Unless programming for a device with limited resources there is seldom a need to utilize bitwise operators, but they can be useful. For instance, the XOR (eXclusive OR) operator lets you exchange values between two variables without the need for a third variable.

xor.c

1. Begin a new program with a preprocessor instruction to include the standard input/output library functions

```
#include <stdio.h>
```

2. Add a main function that declares and initializes two integer variables, then outputs their initial values

```
int main()
{
  int x = 10 , y = 5 ;
  printf( "\nx=%d y=%d\n" , x, y ) ;
}
```

3. Next, in the main function block, insert an XOR statement three times to exchange the variable values by binary bit manipulation

```
x = x ^ y ;     /* 1010 ^ 0101 = 1111 (decimal 15) */
y = x ^ y ;     /* 1111 ^ 0101 = 1010 (decimal 10) */
x = x ^ y ;     /* 1111 ^ 1010 = 0101 (decimal 5)  */
```

4. Now, insert a statement to output the exchanged values

```
printf( "\nx=%d y=%d\n" , x, y ) ;
```

5. At the end of the main function block, return a zero integer value, as required by the function declaration

```
return 0 ;
```

6. Save the program file, then compile and execute the program to see the XOR bitwise magic

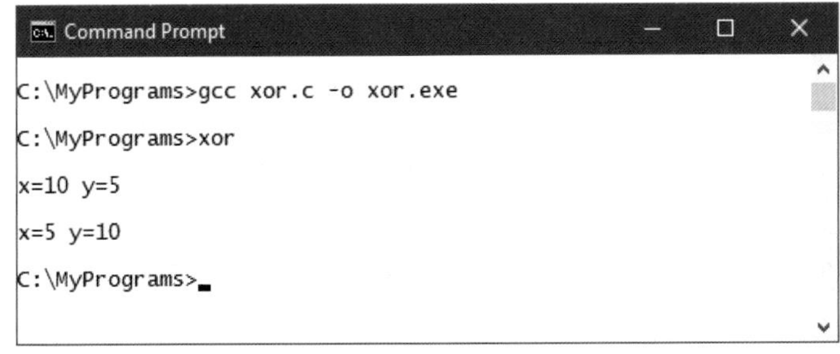

Command Prompt
C:\MyPrograms>gcc xor.c -o xor.exe
C:\MyPrograms>xor
x=10 y=5
x=5 y=10
C:\MyPrograms>

Do not confuse bitwise operators with logical operators. Bitwise operators compare binary numbers whereas logical operators evaluate Boolean values.

Flagging bits

By far the most common use of bitwise operators is to manipulate a compact "bit field" containing a set of Boolean "flags". This is a much more efficient use of memory than storing Boolean flag values in separate variables – a **char** data type of just 1 byte can hold a bit field of eight flags, one per bit, whereas eight separate **char** variables would require 8 whole bytes of memory.

The initial bit flags can be set by assigning a decimal value to the variable whose binary equivalent has a **1** for each bit that is to be turned "on" as a Boolean flag. For example, decimal 8 has a binary equivalent of **1000** (1x8 0x4 0x2 0x1) so turns on the fourth flag, reading from right to left from the least significant bit.

Subsequently, the bit flag values can be reversed using the bitwise NOT ~ operator but care must be taken to mask zeros before the bit flags, otherwise they will each be returned as **1**. For example, to reverse a bit field of four flags within the four right bits of a byte, the four left bits must be masked. Decimal 15 is binary **0001111** (0x128 0x64 0x32 0x16 1x8 1x4 1x2 1x1) and can be applied as this mask with the bitwise AND **&** operator.

The bit flag pattern can also be manipulated by shifting those flags that are turned on by a specified number of bits, using the bitwise Shift left **<<** and Shift right **>>** operators.

bitflag.c

1. Begin a new program with a preprocessor instruction to include the standard input/output library functions

```
#include <stdio.h>
```

2. Add a main function that declares a character variable initialized with a decimal value turning on one bit flag

```
int main()
{
  int flags = 8 ; /* Binary 1000 (1x8 0x4 0x2 0x1) */
}
```

3. Next, in the main function block, assign a new value to the variable, to also turn on another flag

```
flags = flags | 2 ; /* 1000 | 0010 = 1010 (decimal 10) */
```

4 Now, insert statements to output all the bit flag settings

```
printf( "Flag 1: %s\n" , ( (flags & 1) > 0) ? "ON" : "OFF") ;
printf( "Flag 2: %s\n" , ( (flags & 2) > 0) ? "ON" : "OFF") ;
printf( "Flag 3: %s\n" , ( (flags & 4) > 0) ? "ON" : "OFF") ;
printf( "Flag 4: %s\n\n" , ((flags & 8) > 0) ? "ON" : "OFF") ;
```

5 Next, insert statements to mask the first four bits of the byte, then flip all the bit flag settings

```
char mask = 15 ;          /* Binary 00001111 */
flags = ~flags & mask ;  /* ~(1010 & 1111=1010)= 0101 */
```

6 Now, insert statements to output the reversed bit flag settings and the decimal value representing this pattern

```
printf( "Flag 1: %s\n" , ( (flags & 1) > 0) ? "ON" : "OFF") ;
printf( "Flag 2: %s\n" , ( (flags & 2) > 0) ? "ON" : "OFF") ;
printf( "Flag 3: %s\n" , ( (flags & 4) > 0) ? "ON" : "OFF") ;
printf( "Flag 4: %s\n\n" , ((flags & 8) > 0) ? "ON" : "OFF") ;
printf( "Flags decimal value is %d\n" , flags ) ;
```

7 Add a statement to shift the "on" bit flags one bit to the left then output the decimal value of the new pattern

```
flags = flags << 1 ;      /* 0101 << 1 = 1010. */
printf( "Flags decimal value is now %d\n" , flags ) ;
```

8 At the end of the main function block, return a zero integer value, as required by the function declaration

```
return 0 ;
```

9 Save the program file, then compile and execute the program to see the bit flag manipulation

```
Command Prompt
C:\MyPrograms>gcc bitflag.c -o bitflag.exe

C:\MyPrograms>bitflag
Flag 1: OFF
Flag 2: ON
Flag 3: OFF
Flag 4: ON

Flag 1: ON
Flag 2: OFF
Flag 3: ON
Flag 4: OFF

Flags decimal value is 5
Flags decimal value is now 10

C:\MyPrograms>
```

It's often convenient to predefine constants to represent each bit flag. For example:
#define FLAG1 1
#define FLAG2 2
#define FLAG3 4
#define FLAG4 8

Larger bit fields with more bit flags can be created using a variable with more memory – an **int** data type of 4 bytes has 32 bits.

Understanding precedence

Operator precedence defines the order in which C evaluates expressions. For instance, in the expression **a=6+b*3** the order of precedence determines whether the addition or the multiplication is completed first.

The table below lists operator precedence in decreasing order, where operators on higher rows have precedence over those on lower rows, so their operations get completed first. Operators on the same row have equal precedence but the order of completion is determined by associativity direction. For instance, for "Left to right" associativity the operations on the left get completed first.

The * multiply operator is on a higher row than the + addition operator – so in the expression **a=6+b*3** the multiplication gets completed before the addition operation.

Operator:	Associativity:
( ) Function call **[ ]** Array index **->** Struct pointer **.** Struct member	Left to right
! NOT **~** Bitwise NOT **++** Increment **--** Decrement **+** Positive sign **sizeof** **-** Negative sign ***** Pointer **&** Addressof	Right to left
***** Multiply **/** Divide **%** Modulus	Left to right
+ Add **-** Subtract	Left to right
<< Shift left **>>** Shift right	Left to right
< Less than **<=** Less than or equal to **>** Greater than **>=** Greater than or equal to	Left to right
== Equality **!=** Inequality	Left to right
& Bitwise AND	Left to right
^ Bitwise XOR	Left to right
| Bitwise OR	Left to right
&& AND	Left to right
|| OR	Left to right
?: Conditional	Right to left
= += -= *= /= %= &= ^= |= **<<= >>=** Assignment operators	Right to left
, Comma	Left to right

The **->** and **.** struct operators are described later in this book but are included here to provide a complete precedence table of all operators.

precedence.c

1. Begin a new program with a preprocessor instruction to include the standard input/output library functions

```
#include <stdio.h>
```

2. Add a main function that outputs an integer from an expression following row-level precedence rules, and another following explicitly determined precedence

```
int main()
{
 printf("\nDefault precedence ((2*3)+4)-5 : %d\n", 2*3+4-5 ) ;
 printf("Explicit precedence 2* ((3+4)-5 ): %d\n", 2*((3+4)-5) ) ;
}
```

3. Next, in the main function block, output an integer from following Left-to-right associativity precedence rules then another following explicitly determined precedence

```
printf( "\nDefault precedence (7*3) %% 2: %d\n" , 7*3%2 );
printf( "Explicit precedence 7* (3%%2) : %d\n" , 7*(3%2) ) ;
```

4. Now, output an integer following Right-to-left associativity precedence rules then another from explicit precedence

```
int num = 9 ;
printf("\nDefault precedence(8/2)*4:%d\n", --num/2*sizeof(int));
num = 9 ;
printf("Explicit precedence 8/(2*4):%d\n", --num/(2*sizeof(int)));
```

5. At the end of the main function block, return a zero integer value, as required by the function declaration

```
return 0 ;
```

In order to output a **%** character the **printf()** statement requires **%%**.

6. Save the program file, then compile and execute the program to see output following precedence rules

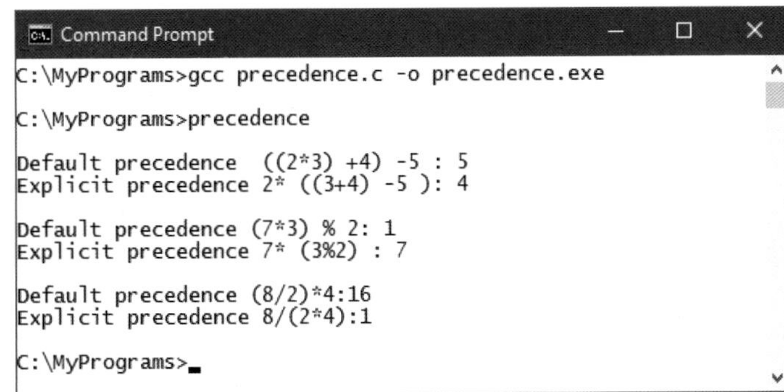

Command Prompt
C:\MyPrograms>gcc precedence.c -o precedence.exe
C:\MyPrograms>precedence
Default precedence ((2*3) +4) -5 : 5
Explicit precedence 2* ((3+4) -5): 4
Default precedence (7*3) % 2: 1
Explicit precedence 7* (3%2) : 7
Default precedence (8/2)*4:16
Explicit precedence 8/(2*4):1
C:\MyPrograms>

Summary

- Arithmetical operators can form expressions with two operands for addition +, subtraction -, multiplication *, division /, and modulus %.
- Increment ++ and decrement -- operators modify a single operand by a value of one.
- The assignment = operator can be combined with an arithmetical operator to perform an arithmetical calculation then assign its result.
- Comparison operators can form expressions comparing two operands for equality ==, inequality !=, greater >, < lesser, greater or equal >=, and lesser or equal <= values.
- Logical AND && and OR || operators form expressions evaluating two operands to return a Boolean value of true or false, but the logical NOT ! operator returns the inverse Boolean value of a single operand.
- A conditional ?: operator evaluates a given Boolean expression then returns one of two operands depending on its result.
- The **sizeof** operator returns the memory byte size of a data type or a data object.
- A single memory byte comprises eight bits, which may each contain a value of one (1) or zero (0).
- Bitwise operators OR |, AND &, NOT ~, and XOR ^ each return a value after comparison of the values within two bits, whereas the Shift left << and Shift right >> operators move the bit values a specified number of bits in their direction.
- The most common use of bitwise operators is to manipulate a compact bit field containing a set of Boolean flags.
- Expressions containing multiple operators will execute their operations in accordance with the default precedence rules unless explicitly determined by the addition of parentheses.

5 Making Statements

This chapter demonstrates how statements can evaluate expressions to determine the direction in which a C program should proceed.

72 Testing expressions

74 Branching switches

76 Looping for a number

78 Looping while true

80 Breaking out of loops

82 Going to labels

84 Summary

Testing expressions

The **if** keyword is used to perform the basic conditional test that evaluates a given expression for a Boolean value of true or false. Statements within braces following the evaluation will only be executed when the expression is found to be true. So, the syntax of an **if** test statement looks like this:

if (***test-expression*** **) {** ***statements-to-execute-when-true*** **}**

There may be multiple statements to be executed when the test is true, but each statement must be terminated by a semi-colon.

Sometimes it may be desirable to evaluate multiple expressions to determine whether following statements should be executed, and this can be achieved in two ways. The logical **&&** AND operator can be used to ensure the statements will only be executed when two expressions are both found to be true, with this syntax:

if ((***test-expression*** **) && (** ***test-expression*** **)) {** ***statements-to-execute*** **}**

When the code to be executed is just a single statement the braces may optionally be omitted.

Alternatively, multiple **if** statements can be "nested", one inside another, to ensure following statements will only be executed when both evaluated expressions are found to be true, like this:

```
if ( test-expression )
{
  if ( test-expression ) { statements-to-execute }
}
```

When one or more expressions evaluated by an **if** test statement is found to be false, the statements within its following braces are not executed and the program proceeds to subsequent code.

It is often preferable to extend an **if** statement by appending an **else** statement specifying statements within braces to be executed when the expressions evaluated by the **if** statement are found to be false, with this syntax:

```
if ( test-expression )
        { statements-to-execute-when-true }
else
        { statements-to-execute-when-false }
```

Multiple expressions can be evaluated by combining **if** and **else** statements with **if() { ... } else if () { ... }**.

This is a fundamental programming technique that offers the program two directions in which to proceed, depending on the result of the evaluation, and is known as "conditional branching".

ifelse.c

1. Begin a new program with a preprocessor instruction to include the standard input/output library functions
```
#include <stdio.h>
```

2. Add a main function that outputs a statement when a tested expression is found to be true
```
int main()
{
  if( 5 > 1 ) { printf( "Yes, 5 is greater than 1\n" ) ; }
}
```

3. Next, in the main function block, output a statement when two tested expressions are both found to be true
```
if( 5 > 1 )
{
  if( 7 > 2 )
  { printf("5 is greater than 1 and 7 is greater than 2\n") ; }
}
```

4. Now, output a default statement after two tested expressions are both found to be false
```
if( 1 > 2 )
{ printf( "1st expression is true\n" ) ; }
else if( 1 > 3 )
{ printf( "2nd expression is true\n" ) ; }
else
{ printf( "Both expressions are false\n" ) ; }
```

5. At the end of the main function block, return a zero integer value, as required by the function declaration
```
return 0 ;
```

6. Save the program file, then compile and execute the program to see output following conditional tests

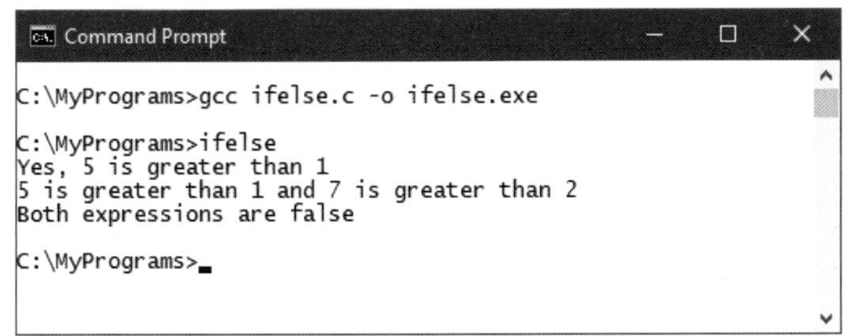
```
C:\MyPrograms>gcc ifelse.c -o ifelse.exe

C:\MyPrograms>ifelse
Yes, 5 is greater than 1
5 is greater than 1 and 7 is greater than 2
Both expressions are false

C:\MyPrograms>
```

In C, Boolean true is represented numerically as 1 and Boolean false a 0 (zero). So the expression **(5 > 1)** is shorthand for **(5 > 1 == 1)**.

Branching switches

Conditional branching performed by multiple **if else** statements can often be performed more efficiently by a **switch** statement when the test expression just evaluates a single condition.

The **switch** statement works in an unusual way. It takes a given value as its parameter argument then seeks to match that value from a number of **case** statements. Code to be executed when a match is found is included in each **case** statement.

It is important to end each **case** statement with a **break** keyword statement so the **switch** statement will then exit when a match is found without seeking further matches – unless that is the deliberate requirement.

Optionally, the list of **case** statements can be followed by a single final **default** statement to specify code to be executed in the event that no matches are found within any of the **case** statements. So the syntax of a switch statement typically looks like this:

```
switch ( test-value )
{
  case match-value : statements-to-execute-when-matched ; break ;
  case match-value : statements-to-execute-when-matched ; break ;
  case match-value : statements-to-execute-when-matched ; break ;
  default : statements-to-execute-when-no-match-found ;
}
```

A **switch** statement can have up to at least 257 case statements according to the ANSI C standard, but no two of its **case** statements can attempt to match the same value.

Where a number of match-values are to each execute the same statements, only the final **case** statement need include the statements to be executed and the **break** statement to exit the **switch** statement block. For example, to output the same message for match-values of 0, 1, and 2:

```
switch ( num )
{
  case 0 :
  case 1 :
  case 2 : printf( "Less than 3\n" ) ; break ;
  case 3 : printf( "Exactly 3\n" ) ; break ;
  default : printf( "Greater than 3 or less than zero\n" ) ;
}
```

Hot tip

It's always a good idea to include a **default** statement – even if it's only to output an error message when the **switch** statement fails.

A **default** statement need not appear at the end of the **switch** block but it is logical to place it there where it needs no **break** statement.

switch.c

1. Begin a new program with a preprocessor instruction to include the standard input/output library functions
```
#include <stdio.h>
```

2. Add a main function that declares and initializes one integer variable and one character variable
```
int main()
{
  int num = 2 ; char letter = 'b' ;
}
```

3. Next, in the main function block, insert a switch statement that attempts to match the integer value
```
switch( num )
{
  case 1 : printf( "Number is one\n" ) ; break ;
  case 2 : printf( "Number is two\n" ) ; break ;
  case 3 : printf( "Number is three\n" ) ; break ;
  default : printf( "Number is unrecognized\n" ) ;
}
```

4. Now, insert a switch statement that attempts to match the character value
```
switch( letter )
{
  case 'a' : case 'b' : case 'c' :
  printf( "Letter is %c\n" , letter ) ; break ;
  default : printf( "Letter is unrecognized\n" ) ;
}
```

5. At the end of the main function block, return a zero integer value, as required by the function declaration
```
return 0 ;
```

6. Save the program file, then compile and execute the program to see output from the switch statements

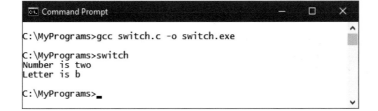

```
Command Prompt

C:\MyPrograms>gcc switch.c -o switch.exe

C:\MyPrograms>switch
Number is two
Letter is b

C:\MyPrograms>_
```

In **switch** statements the **case** keyword, match-value, and colon character are regarded as a unique "label".

Looping for a number

A loop is a piece of code in a program that automatically repeats. One complete execution of all statements within a loop is called an "iteration", or a "pass". The length of a loop is controlled by a conditional test made within the loop. While the tested expression is found to be true, the loop will continue – until the tested expression is found to be false, at which point the loop ends.

In C programming there are three types of loop structure – **for** loops, **while** loops, and **do while** loops. Perhaps the most common of these is the **for** loop, which typically has this syntax:

for (*initializer* ; *test-expression* ; *incrementer*) { *statements* }

The initializer is used to set a starting value for a counter of the number of iterations made by the loop. An integer variable is used for this purpose and is traditionally named "i".

Upon each iteration of the loop the test-expression is evaluated and that iteration will only continue while this expression is true. When the test-expression becomes false the loop ends immediately without executing the statements again. With every iteration the counter is incremented then the statements executed.

Loops can be nested, one within another, to allow complete execution of all iterations of an inner nested loop on each iteration of the outer loop.

forloop.c

1. Begin a new program with a preprocessor instruction to include the standard input/output library functions
```
#include <stdio.h>
```

2. Add a main function that declares two integer variables to be used later as loop iteration counters
```
int main()
{
  int i , j ; }
}
```

3. Next, in the main function block, insert a for loop to output the loop counter value on each of three iterations
```
for( i = 1 ; i < 4 ; i++ )
{
  printf( "Outer loop iteration %d\n" , i ) ;
}
```

4. At the end of the main function block, return a zero integer value, as required by the function declaration
   return 0 ;

5. Save the program file, then compile and execute the program to see output from the for loop

```
Command Prompt
C:\MyPrograms>gcc forloop.c -o forloop.exe

C:\MyPrograms>forloop
Outer loop iteration 1
Outer loop iteration 2
Outer loop iteration 3

C:\MyPrograms>_
```

6. Now, in the loop block, insert a nested loop immediately after the existing output statement, to output the loop counter value on each of three inner loop iterations

```
for( j = 1 ; j < 4 ; j++ )
{
  printf( "\tInner loop iteration %d\n" , j ) ;
}
```

7. Save the program file, then compile and execute the program once more to see output from both loops

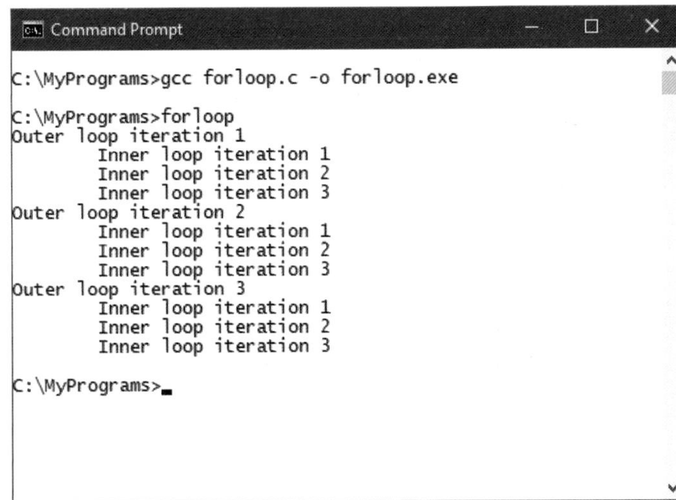
Command Prompt
C:\MyPrograms>gcc forloop.c -o forloop.exe
C:\MyPrograms>forloop
Outer loop iteration 1
Inner loop iteration 1
Inner loop iteration 2
Inner loop iteration 3
Outer loop iteration 2
Inner loop iteration 1
Inner loop iteration 2
Inner loop iteration 3
Outer loop iteration 3
Inner loop iteration 1
Inner loop iteration 2
Inner loop iteration 3
C:\MyPrograms>_

Hot tip

A **for** loop counter can also count down – by decrementing the counter value on each iteration using **i--** instead of **i++**.

Looping while true

A **while** loop is an alternative to the **for** loop described in the previous example. The **while** loop also requires an initializer, test-expression, and an incrementer, but these are not neatly listed within a single pair of parentheses as they are in a **for** loop. Instead, the initializer must appear before the start of the loop block, and the test-expression must appear within parentheses after the **while** keyword, followed by braces containing both an incrementer and the statements to be executed on each iteration.

Notice that a semi-colon terminator is required after the **while** statement in the **do while** loop.

initializer
while (***test-expression*** **)**
{ ***statements-to-be-executed*** **;** ***incrementer*** **}**

A do while loop provides a subtle variation on the syntax above by placing the do keyword before the loop block and moving the while statement to after the loop block:

initializer
do { ***statements-to-be-executed*** **;** ***incrementer*** **}**
while (***test-expression*** **) ;**

Both **while** loops and **do while** loops will proceed to make iterations until the test-expression is found to be false, at which point the loop will exit. It is therefore essential that the loop body contains code that will, at some point, change the result of the test-expression evaluation – otherwise an infinite loop is created that will lock the system.

In the event that a program runs an infinite loop, on Windows or Linux systems press the **Ctrl + C** keyboard keys to halt the loop execution.

The significant difference between a **while** loop and a **do while** loop is that a **while** loop will not make a single iteration if the test-expression is false on its first evaluation. In contrast, a **do while** loop will always make at least one iteration because its statements are executed before the evaluation is made. If this is desirable a **do while** loop is obviously the best choice, otherwise the choice between a **for** loop and a **while** loop is largely a matter of personal preference. One rule of thumb suggests that a **for** loop is best used to perform a specific number of iterations, whereas a **while** loop is best used to iterate until a certain condition is met.

Loops are the perfect partner to use with arrays as each iteration can effortlessly read or write into successive array elements.

dowhile.c

1. Begin a new program with a preprocessor instruction to include the standard input/output library functions

```
#include <stdio.h>
```

2. Add a main function that declares a counter variable then declares and initializes an array variable of three elements

```
int main()
{
  int i , arr[3] = { 10 , 20 , 30 } ;
}
```

3. Next, in the main function block, insert a while loop that outputs each element number and the value it contains

```
i = 0 ;
while( i < 3 )
{
  printf( "While: arr[%d] = %d\n" , i, arr[i] ) ;  i++ ;
}
```

4. Now, insert a do while loop that also outputs each element number and the value it contains

```
i = 0 ;
do
{
  printf( "\nDo while: arr[%d] = %d" , i, arr[i] ) ; i++ ;
}
while( i < 3 ) ;
```

5. At the end of the main function block, return a zero integer value, as required by the function declaration

```
return 0 ;
```

6. Save the program file, then compile and execute the program to see apparently identical output from the loops

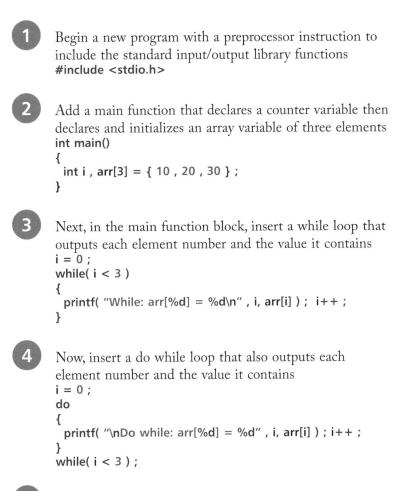

```
Command Prompt
C:\MyPrograms>gcc dowhile.c -o dowhile.exe

C:\MyPrograms>dowhile
While: arr[0] = 10
While: arr[1] = 20
While: arr[2] = 30

Do while: arr[0] = 10
Do while: arr[1] = 20
Do while: arr[2] = 30
C:\MyPrograms>_
```

Change the value in this test-expression to zero – so **while (i<0)** in both loops – then recompile and run the program again to see only the first iteration of the **do while** loop get executed.

Breaking out of loops

The **break** keyword can be used to prematurely terminate a loop when a specified condition is met. The **break** statement is situated inside the loop statement block and is preceded by a test-expression. When the test returns true, the loop ends immediately and the program proceeds on to the next task. For example, in a nested inner loop it proceeds to the next iteration of the outer loop.

breakcontinue.c

1. Begin a new program with a preprocessor instruction to include the standard input/output library functions

```
#include <stdio.h>
```

2. Add a main function that declares two integer variables to be used later as loop iteration counters

```
int main()
{
  int i , j ;
}
```

3. Next, in the main function block, insert two nested loops to output their counter values on each of three iterations

```
for( i = 1 ; i < 4 ; i++ )
{
  for( j = 1 ; j < 4; j++ )
  {
    printf( "Running i=%d j=%d\n", i, j ) ;
  }
}
```

4. At the end of the main function block, return a zero integer value, as required by the function declaration

```
return 0 ;
```

5. Save the program file, then compile and execute the program to see the output from nested loops

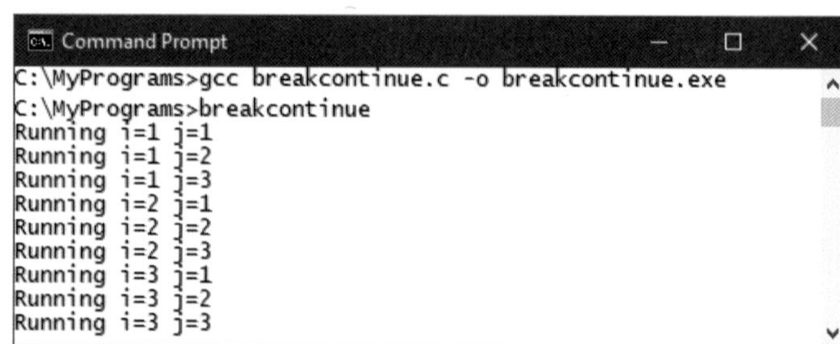
Command Prompt
C:\MyPrograms>gcc breakcontinue.c -o breakcontinue.exe
C:\MyPrograms>breakcontinue
Running i=1 j=1
Running i=1 j=2
Running i=1 j=3
Running i=2 j=1
Running i=2 j=2
Running i=2 j=3
Running i=3 j=1
Running i=3 j=2
Running i=3 j=3

6 Now, insert this **break** statement at the very beginning of the inner loop block, to break out of the inner loop – then save, compile, and run the program once more

```
if( i == 2 && j == 1 )
{
  printf( "Breaks inner loop when i=%d and j=%d\n" , i, j ) ;
  break ;
}
```

Don't forget

Here the **break** statement halts all three iterations of the inner loop when the outer loop tries to run it the second time.

```
Command Prompt
C:\MyPrograms>breakcontinue
Running i=1 j=1
Running i=1 j=2
Running i=1 j=3
Breaks inner loop when i=2 and j=1
Running i=3 j=1
Running i=3 j=2
Running i=3 j=3

C:\MyPrograms>
```

The **continue** keyword can be used to skip a single iteration of a loop when a specified condition is met. The **continue** statement is situated inside the loop statement block and is preceded by a test expression. When the test returns true, that single iteration ends.

7

Insert this **continue** statement at the beginning of the inner loop block, to skip the first iteration of the inner loop – then save, compile, and run the program again

```
if( i == 1 && j == 1 )
{
  printf( "Continues inner loop when i=%d and j=%d\n", i, j ) ;
  continue;
}
```

Don't forget

Here the **continue** statement just skips the first iteration of the inner loop when the outer loop tries to run it for the first time.

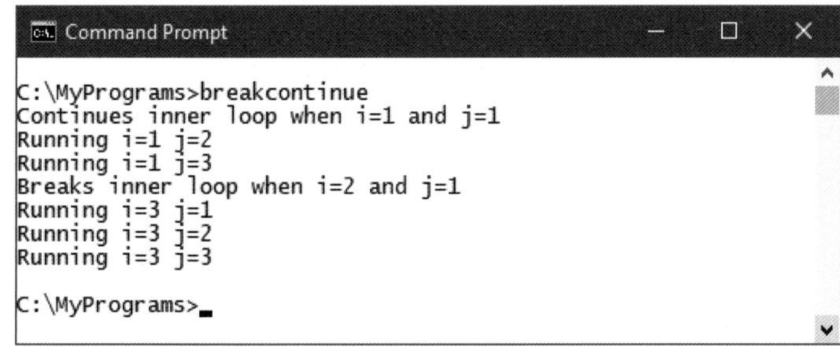
Command Prompt
C:\MyPrograms>breakcontinue
Continues inner loop when i=1 and j=1
Running i=1 j=2
Running i=1 j=3
Breaks inner loop when i=2 and j=1
Running i=3 j=1
Running i=3 j=2
Running i=3 j=3
C:\MyPrograms>

Going to labels

The **goto** keyword supposedly allows the program flow to jump to labels at other points in the program code, much like a hyperlink on a web page. However, in reality this can cause errors; its use is frowned upon; and it is considered bad programming practice.

The **goto** keyword jump is a powerful feature that has existed in computer programs for decades, but its power was abused by many early programmers who created programs that jumped around in an unfathomable manner. This produced unreadable program code, so the use of **goto** became hugely unpopular.

One possible valid use of the **goto** keyword is to break cleanly from an inner nested loop by jumping to a label just after the end of its outer loop block. This immediately exits both loops so no further iterations of either loop are executed.

jump.c

1. Begin a new program with a preprocessor instruction to include the standard input/output library functions

```
#include <stdio.h>
```

2. Add a main function that declares two integer variables to be used later as loop iteration counters

```
int main()
{
  int i , j ;
}
```

3. Next, in the main function block, insert two nested loops to output their counter values on each of three iterations

```
for( i = 1 ; i < 4 ; i++ )
{
  for( j = 1 ; j < 4 ; j++ )
  {
    printf( "Running i=%d j=%d\n", i, j ) ;
  }
}
```

4. Insert a statement as the first line of the inner nested loop, to jump to a label named “end” at a specified counter value

```
if( i == 2 && j == 1 ) { goto end ; }
```

5. Now, add the label after the closing brace of the outer loop

```
} end:
```

Notice that the **goto** statement specifies the label by name only, but the label itself must have a terminating : colon.

...cont'd

6. At the end of the main function block, return a zero integer value, as required by the function declaration
return 0 ;

7. Save the program file, then compile and execute the program to see the loops exit after the jump

In C, Boolean values are represented numerically as 1 (true) and 0 (false).

One alternative, avoiding the **goto** keyword, might be to check a variable for a Boolean true value (1) on each iteration of each loop:

8. Add another variable to the existing variable declarations and initialize with a true value of one
int i , j , flag = 1 ;

9. Insert a conditional test of the new variable's value, both at the start of the outer loop block and at the start of the inner loop block just before the output statement
if(flag)

10. Change the first line of the inner loop to replace the goto statement with one assigning a false value of zero
if(i == 2 && j == 1) { flag = 0 ; }

11. Delete the now obsolete **end:** label after the closing brace then save, compile, and execute the program again to see the same resulting output as before

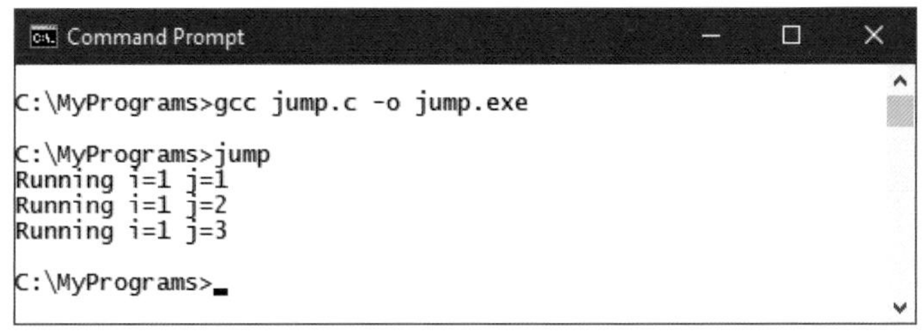

Command Prompt
C:\MyPrograms>gcc jump.c -o jump.exe
C:\MyPrograms>jump
Running i=1 j=1
Running i=1 j=2
Running i=1 j=3
C:\MyPrograms>_

Avoid creating a program executable named "goto.exe" as this would conflict with the internal Windows **GOTO** command.

Summary

- The **if** keyword performs a basic conditional test to evaluate a given expression for a Boolean value of true or false.
- The **else** keyword can be used to provide alternative statements to execute when an **if** statement evaluates an expression as false.
- Offering a program alternative directions in which to proceed following an evaluation is known as "conditional branching".
- Conditional branching performed by multiple **if else** statements can often be performed more efficiently by a **switch** statement.
- Usually, the **case** statements within a **switch** block must each be terminated by a **break** statement.
- Optionally, a **switch** block may contain a **default** statement specifying statements to execute when no match is found.
- The **for** keyword is followed by parentheses specifying an initializer, test-expression, and incrementer to control a loop.
- The **while** keyword is followed by parentheses specifying a test expression to determine whether a loop should continue.
- A **while** loop block must be preceded by an initializer and contain an incrementer within its statement block.
- The **do** keyword is followed by a statement block after which there must be a **while** statement terminated by a semi-colon.
- A **do while** loop must be preceded by an initializer and contain an incrementer within its statement block.
- Unlike **for** loops and **while** loops, the statements in a **do while** loop will always be executed at least once.
- The **break** keyword can be used to terminate a loop, whereas the **continue** keyword can be used to skip a single iteration.
- Loops may be nested and the **goto** keyword can be used to exit to a specified label, although its use is not recommended.

6 Employing Functions

This chapter demonstrates how statements can be enclosed within a "function" for execution whenever called by the C program.

86 Declaring functions
88 Supplying arguments
90 Calling recursively
92 Placing functions in headers
94 Restricting accessibility
96 Summary

Declaring functions

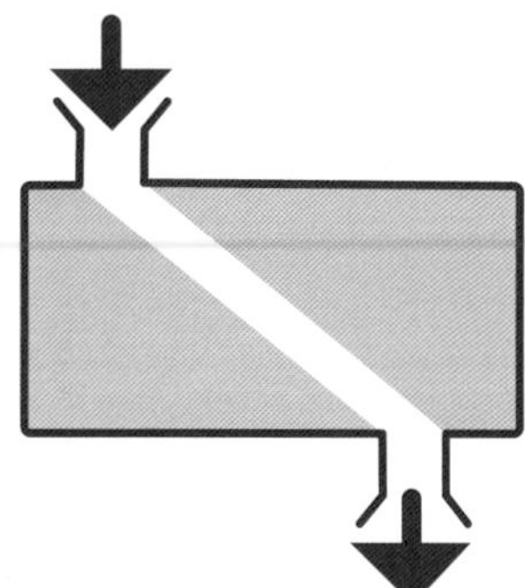

Previous examples in this book have used the obligatory **main()** function and standard functions contained in the C header library, such as the **printf()** function from the **stdio.h** file. However, most C programs contain a number of custom functions, which can be called as required during the execution of the program.

A function block simply contains a group of statements that get executed whenever that function is called. Once the function statements have been executed, program flow resumes at the point directly following the function call. This modularity is very useful in C programming to isolate set routines so they can be called upon repeatedly.

To introduce a custom function into a C program it must first be declared, in a similar manner that variables must be declared before they can be used. Function declarations should be added before the **main()** function block.

Like the **main()** function, custom functions can return a value. The data type of this return value must be included in the function declaration. If the function is to return no value, its return data type should be declared with the **void** keyword. The function should be named following the same naming conventions used for variable names.

The function prototype is sometimes referred to as the "function header".

The function declaration is more correctly known as the "function prototype" and simply informs the compiler about the function. The actual function definition, which includes the statements to be executed, appears after the **main()** function. The custom function can then be called upon to execute its statements from within the **main()** function, as required.

If a custom function returns a value this can be assigned to a variable of an appropriate data type, or simply displayed as output using the appropriate format specifier.

first.c

1. Begin a new program with a preprocessor instruction to include the standard input/output library functions

```
#include <stdio.h>
```

2. Declare three custom function prototypes

```
void first() ;
int square5() ;
int cube5() ;
```

3. Add a main function that declares an integer variable

```
int main()
{
  int num ;
}
```

4. After the main function, define the custom functions

```
void first()
{
  printf( "Hello from the first function\n" ) ;
}

int square5()
{
  int square = 5 * 5 ;
  return square ;
}

int cube5()
{
  int cube = ( 5 * 5 ) * 5 ;
  return cube ;
}
```

5. Now, insert calls to the custom functions in the main function block

```
first() ;
num = square5() ;
printf( "5x5= %d\n" , num ) ;
printf( "5x5x5= %d\n" , cube5() ) ;
```

6. At the end of the main function block, return a zero integer value, as required by that function declaration

```
return 0 ;
```

7. Save the program file, then compile and execute the program to see the output from custom functions

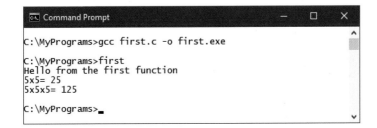

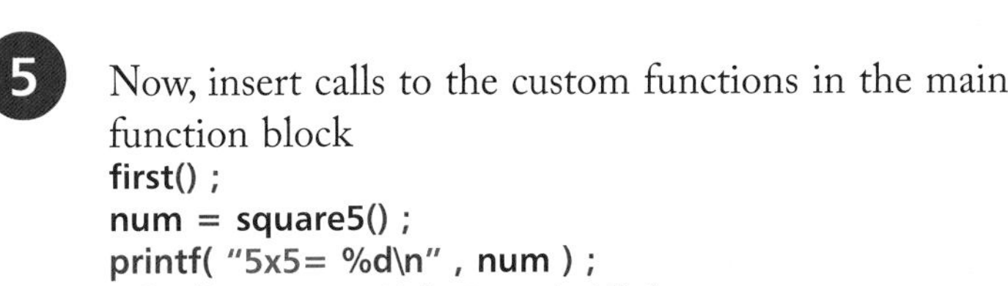

Notice that each function prototype must end with a semi-colon.

The custom function definitions could technically appear before the **main()** function – but convention is to include prototypes and keep the **main()** function at the beginning of the program code.

Supplying arguments

Data can be passed as "arguments" to custom functions, which can then use that data to execute their statements. The function prototype must include the name and data type of each argument.

Don't forget

Passing data "by value" assigns the value to a variable in the called function. The function can then manipulate that copy but it does not affect the original data.

It is important to recognize that in C programming, the data is passed "by value" to the variable specified as the function argument. This is different to some other programming languages, such as Pascal, whose arguments are passed "by reference" – where the function operates on the original value, not just a local copy.

The arguments in a function prototype are known as the "formal parameters" of the function. These may be of different data types, and multiple arguments can be specified for a single function if separated by a comma. For example, a function prototype with arguments of each of the four data types could look like this:

```
void action( char c , int i , float f , double d ) ;
```

The compiler checks that the formal parameters specified in the function prototype match those in the function definition and will report an error if they do not match.

args.c

1. Begin a new program with a preprocessor instruction to include the standard input/output library functions

```
#include <stdio.h>
```

2. Declare three custom function prototypes with one argument to be passed to each one when called

```
void display( char str[] ) ;
int square( int x ) ;
int cube( int y ) ;
```

3. Add a main function that declares an integer variable and a character array variable initialized with a string of text

```
int main()
{
  int num ;
  char msg[50] = "String to be passed to a function" ;
}
```

4. After the main function, define the custom functions

```
void display( char str[] )
{
  printf( "%s\n" , str ) ;
}

int square( int x )
{
  return ( x * x ) ;
}

int cube( int y )
{
  return ( y * y ) * y ;
}
```

5. Now, in the main function, insert statements calling each of the custom functions and passing argument values

```
display( msg ) ;
num = square( 4 ) ;
printf( "4x4= %d\n" , num ) ;
printf( "4x4x4= %d\n" , cube( 4 ) ) ;
```

6. At the end of the main function block, return a zero integer value, as required by the function declaration

```
return 0 ;
```

7. Save the program file, then compile and execute the program to see the output from custom functions using passed argument values

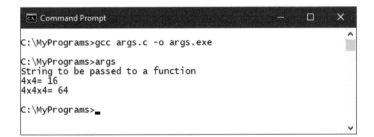

```
Command Prompt

C:\MyPrograms>gcc args.c -o args.exe

C:\MyPrograms>args
String to be passed to a function
4x4= 16
4x4x4= 64

C:\MyPrograms>_
```

The argument names used in the function definition can differ from those used in the function prototype but the argument data types, number, and order must be the same. It is clearer to adopt the same names in both, though.

A function need not return any value but can still include the **return** keyword without any following value to signify the return of control to the caller.

Calling recursively

Statements within custom functions can freely call other custom functions just as readily as they can call standard library functions like **printf()**.

Additionally, functions can call themselves, and these are known as “recursive functions”. As with loops it is important that recursive functions must modify a tested expression to avoid continuous execution – so the function call ends at some point.

recur.c

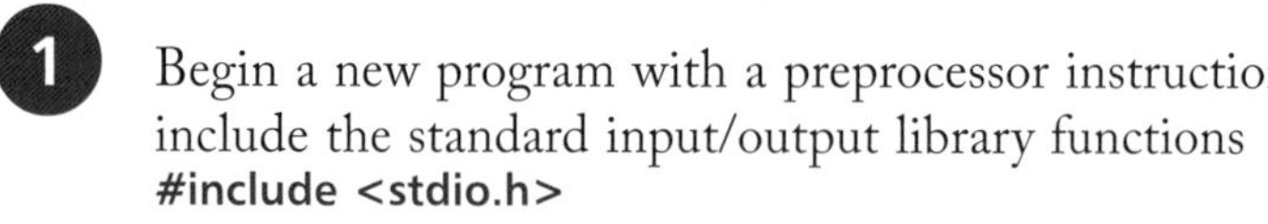

1. Begin a new program with a preprocessor instruction to include the standard input/output library functions

```
#include <stdio.h>
```

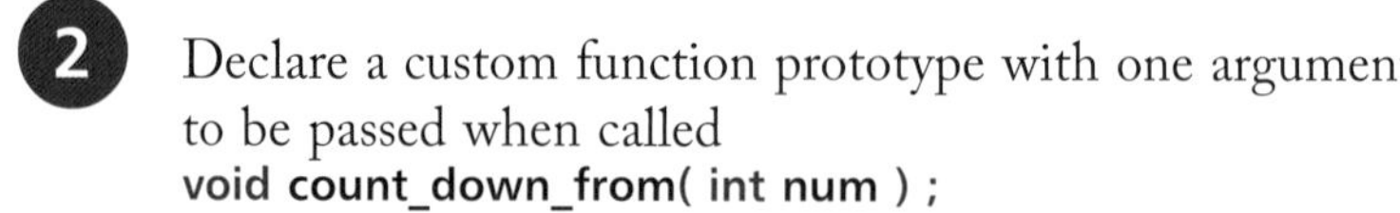

2. Declare a custom function prototype with one argument to be passed when called

```
void count_down_from( int num ) ;
```

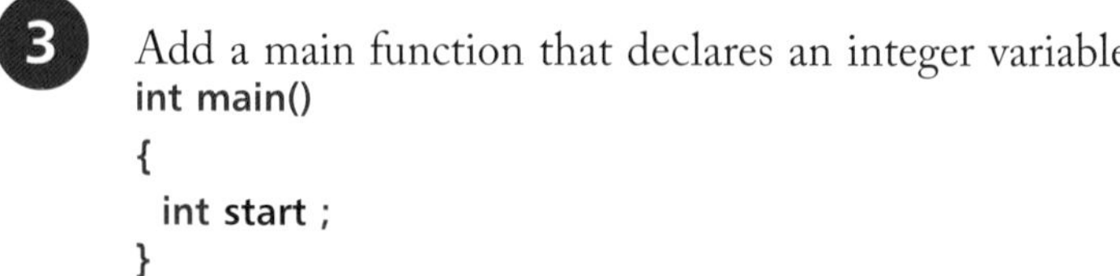

3. Add a main function that declares an integer variable

```
int main()
{
  int start ;
}
```

4. Next, in the main function block, add a statement requesting the user input an integer value to be assigned to the variable

```
printf( "Enter a positive integer to count down from: " ) ;
scanf( "%d" , &start ) ;
```

5. Now, in the main function block, add a call to the custom function, passing it the value entered by the user

```
count_down_from( start ) ;
```

6. In the main function block, add a statement to output a message when control returns from the custom function

```
printf( "Lift Off!\n" ) ;
```

7. At the end of the main function block, return a zero integer value, as required by the function declaration

```
return 0 ;
```

The variable name must be preceded by the **&** addressof operator in the **scanf()** function, as described on page 24.

8. After the main function block, begin the custom function definition with a statement to output the argument value passed during the function call

```
void count_down_from( int num )
{
  printf( "%d\n" , num ) ;
}
```

9. Next, in the custom function block, decrement the value passed as the argument

```
--num ;
```

10. Now, in the custom function block, add a conditional test to return control to the main function if the decremented value is below zero or pass it as an argument in a recursive call to this function

```
if( num  < 0 ) return ;
else
count_down_from( num ) ;
```

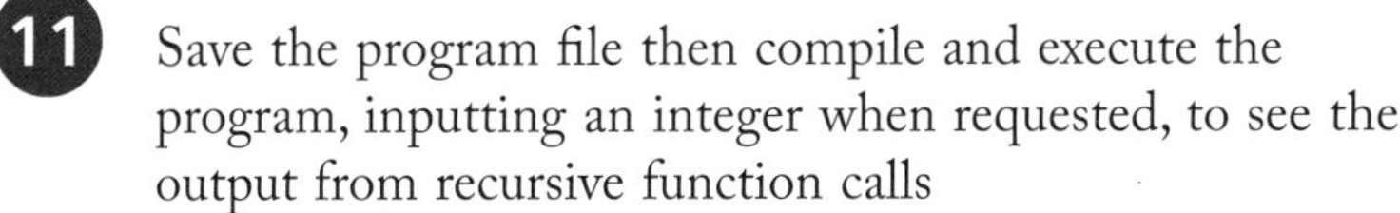

11. Save the program file then compile and execute the program, inputting an integer when requested, to see the output from recursive function calls

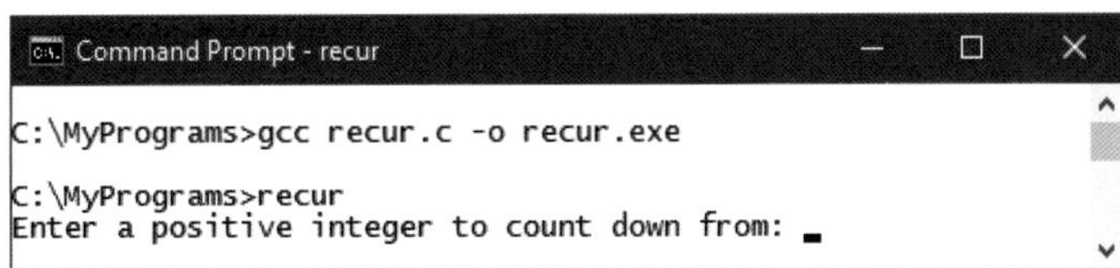

Command Prompt - recur
C:\MyPrograms>gcc recur.c -o recur.exe
C:\MyPrograms>recur
Enter a positive integer to count down from:

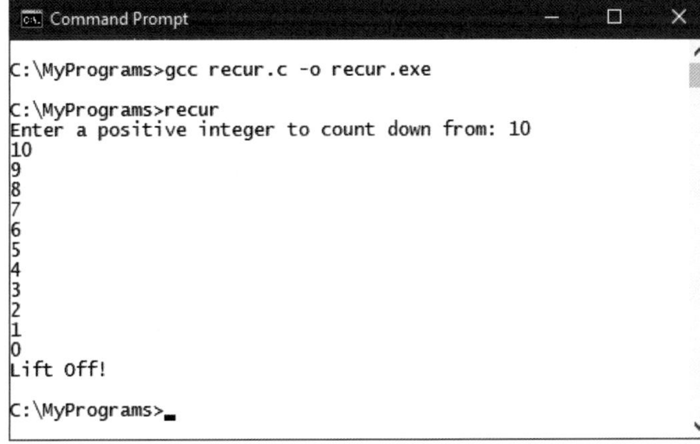

Command Prompt
C:\MyPrograms>gcc recur.c -o recur.exe
C:\MyPrograms>recur
Enter a positive integer to count down from: 10
10
9
8
7
6
5
4
3
2
1
0
Lift Off!
C:\MyPrograms>

A recursive function can be less efficient than using a loop.

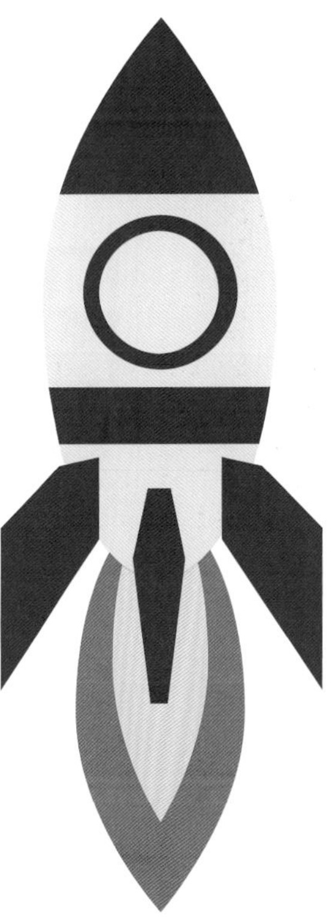

Placing functions in headers

The example programs listed throughout this book are necessarily small due to space considerations but in reality, most C programs will contain significantly more code.

When developing larger programs, some thought should be given to program structure. Maintaining the entire program code in a single file can become unwieldy as the program grows.

In order to simplify the program structure, a custom header file can be created to contain functions that may be used repeatedly. This should be named with a ".h" file extension, like the standard header files in the C library.

The functions in the custom header file can be made available to the program by adding an **#include** preprocessor directive at the start of the file containing the **main()** function. The custom header file name should be enclosed within double quotes in the preprocessor directive though, rather than by the < and > angled brackets that are used to include standard header files.

utils.h

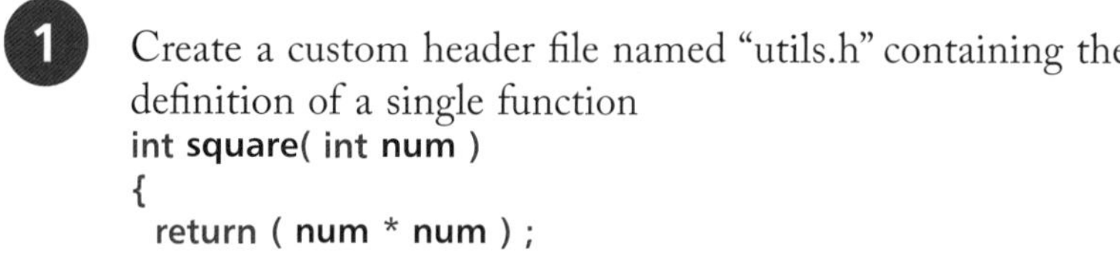

1. Create a custom header file named "utils.h" containing the definition of a single function

```
int square( int num )
{
  return ( num * num ) ;
}
```

square.c

2. Begin a new program with a preprocessor instruction to include the standard input/output library functions and the custom header file

```
#include <stdio.h>
#include "utils.h"
```

3. Declare a custom function prototype with no arguments

```
void getnum() ;
```

4. Add a main function to call the other function then return a zero integer as required by the declaration

```
int main()
{
  getnum() ;
  return 0 ;
}
```

5. After the main function block, begin the second function definition by declaring two variables

```
void getnum()
{
  int num ;
  char again ;
}
```

The program file and custom header file must be located in the same directory but are compiled with the usual command – the compiler reads the header file automatically because of the **#include** directive.

6. Next, in this function definition, add statements to request user input and assign its value to a variable

```
printf( "Enter an integer to be squared: " ) ;
scanf( "%d" , &num ) ;
```

7. Now, output a result by calling the function in the custom header file, passing it the input value as its argument

```
printf( "%d squared is %d\n" , num, square(num) ) ;
```

8. Add a statement requesting further user input and assign its value to a variable

```
printf( "Square another number? Y or N: " ) ;
scanf( "%1s" , &again ) ;
```

9. Finally, add a conditional test to execute this function once more or return control to the main function

```
if( ( again == 'Y' ) || ( again == 'y' ) ) getnum() ;
else return ;
```

Notice the use of the **%1s** format specifier in this example – to read the next character entered by the user.

10. Save the program file then compile and execute the program, inputting an integer and character when requested, to see the output from the function calls

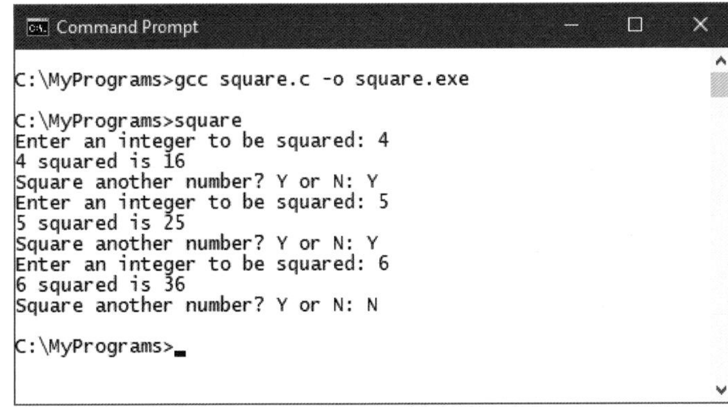

Restricting accessibility

The **static** keyword can be used to restrict the accessibility of functions to the file in which they are created, in exactly the same way that **static** variables have restricted accessibility. This is recommended practice in larger programs that are spread over multiple ".c" files, to safeguard against accidental misuse of functions. For instance, the **square()** and **multiply()** functions can't be directly called from the **main()** function in this example.

menu.c

1. Begin a new program with a preprocessor instruction to include the standard input/output library functions

```
#include <stdio.h>
```

2. Declare two custom function prototypes

```
void menu() ;
void action( int option ) ;
```

3. Add a main function to call the first custom function then return a zero integer as required by the declaration

```
int main()
{
  menu() ;
  return 0 ;
}
```


4. After the main block, define the first custom function to pass a menu option as an argument to another function

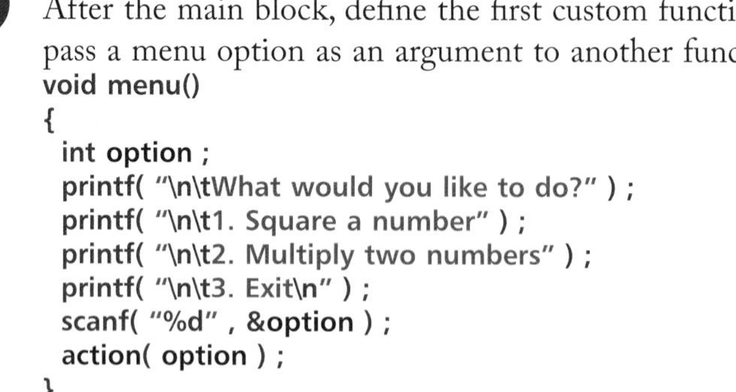

```
void menu()
{
  int option ;
  printf( "\n\tWhat would you like to do?" ) ;
  printf( "\n\t1. Square a number" ) ;
  printf( "\n\t2. Multiply two numbers" ) ;
  printf( "\n\t3. Exit\n" ) ;
  scanf( "%d" , &option ) ;
  action( option ) ;
}
```

Notice that prototypes are declared here for each file containing calls to those functions – to prevent an "implicit declaration of function" compiler warning.

action.c

5. Begin a second program file with a preprocessor to include the standard input/output functions, and declare the custom prototypes once more

```
#include <stdio.h>

void menu() ;
void action( int option ) ;
```

6. Now, define two simple static functions

```
static int square( int a ) { return (a * a) ; }
static int multiply( int a, int b ){ return a * b ; }
```

7. Finally, define the function being passed the menu option from the call in the main function to execute an appropriate action – calling upon the static functions created in this file when required

```
void action( int option )
{
  int n1 , n2 ;
  if( option == 1 )
  {
    printf( "Enter an integer to be squared: " ) ;
    scanf( "%d", &n1 ) ;
    printf( "%d x %d = %d \n" , n1 , n1 , square(n1) ) ;
    menu() ;
  }
  else if( option == 2 )
  {
    printf( "Enter two integers to multiply " ) ;
    printf( "separated by a space: " ) ;
    scanf( "%d" , &n1) ; scanf( "%d" , &n2 ) ;
    printf( "%d x %d = %d\n", n1, n2, multiply( n1, n2 ) ) ;
    menu() ;
  }
  else return ;
}
```

8. Save both program files, then compile and execute the program to see the output returned from static functions

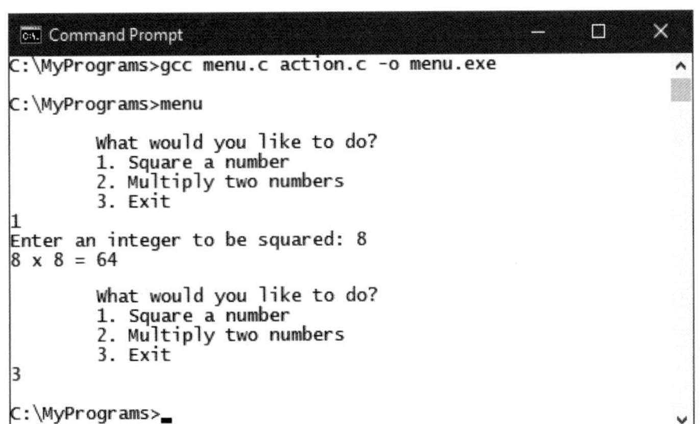

An example demonstrating static variables can be found on page 28.

Note that the compiler command specifies both .c source code file names to create a single executable file.

Summary

- Custom functions are declared by stating that function's return data type, then its name followed by parentheses, and ending with a semi-colon.
- Function declarations are also known as "function prototypes" and should appear before the main function – so the compiler knows of their existence when reading the **main()** function.
- Function definitions, containing the actual statements to be executed when that function is called, should appear after the **main()** function block.
- Function declarations may optionally include within their parentheses a comma-separated list of arguments to be passed to the function by its caller, each stating a data type and name.
- Arguments specified in a function definition must match those of its declaration, as these are its formal parameters.
- In C programming, arguments are passed by value – so the function operates on a copy of the original value.
- A function may call itself recursively, but must include a statement to modify a tested expression to exit at some point.
- Custom header files have a ".h" file extension.
- The preprocessor directive to **#include** a custom header file must specify its file name enclosed within double quotes.
- The **static** keyword can be used in function declarations and definitions to restrict accessibility by reducing their scope to the file in which they appear.
- Larger programs should declare functions as **static** unless there is some specific reason they must be visible outside their file.
- Function prototypes are not required for functions outside the file containing the **main()** function.

7 Pointing to Data

This chapter demonstrates how data in a C program can be referenced by pointing to the machine address at which it is stored.

98 Accessing data via pointers
100 Doing pointer arithmetic
102 Passing pointers to functions
104 Creating arrays of pointers
106 Pointing to functions
108 Summary

Accessing data via pointers

Pointers are a very useful part of efficient C programming. They are variables that store the memory address of other variables.

When a regular variable is declared, memory is allocated, of the size appropriate for its data type, at a vacant memory address. Subsequently, wherever the program finds that variable name, it references the data stored at that memory address. Similarly, wherever the program finds the name of a pointer variable, it references the address it stores. But a pointer variable can be "dereferenced" to reveal the data stored at the address it contains.

The * dereference operator is alternatively known as the "indirection" operator.

Pointer variables are declared in just the same way that other variables are declared but the variable name is prefixed by a "*" . In this case, the * character represents the "dereference operator" and merely denotes that the declared variable is a pointer. The pointer's data type must match the data type of the variable to which it points.

Once declared, a pointer variable can be assigned the address of another variable using the **&** addressof operator. The pointer variable should not be prefixed by the * dereference operator in the assignment statement unless the pointer is initialized immediately in the pointer variable declaration itself.

- A pointer variable name, when used alone, references a memory address expressed in hexadecimal.

Be sure to also delete the pointer when deleting the object to which it refers so as not to leave a "dangling pointer" in the program.

When the * dereference operator is used in a variable declaration it merely denotes that the variable is a pointer, but prefixing a variable pointer name with the * dereference operator elsewhere in the program references the data stored at the address assigned to that pointer variable.

- A pointer variable name, when prefixed by the * dereference operator after its declaration, references the data stored at the address assigned to that pointer variable.

This means that a program can get the address assigned to a pointer variable just using its name, or it can get the data stored at the address to which it points by prefixing its name with the * dereference operator.

point.c

1. Begin a new program with a preprocessor instruction to include the standard input/output library functions

```
#include <stdio.h>
```

2. Add a main function that declares and initializes a regular integer variable and an integer pointer variable

```
int main()
{
  int num = 8 ;
  int *ptr = &num ;
}
```

3. Next, in the main function block, output the contents of both variables and the value dereferenced by the pointer

```
printf( “Regular variable contains: %d\n” , num ) ;
printf( “Pointer variable contains: 0x%p\n” , ptr  ) ;
printf( “Pointer points to value: %d\n\n” , *ptr ) ;
```

4. Now, in the main function block, assign a new value to the regular variable via the pointer variable, then output the contents and dereferenced value once more

```
*ptr = 12 ;
printf( “Regular variable contains: %d\n” , num ) ;
printf( “Pointer variable contains: 0x%p\n” , ptr  ) ;
printf( “Pointer points to value: %d\n\n” , *ptr ) ;
```

5. At the end of the main function block, return a zero integer value, as required by the function declaration

```
return 0 ;
```

6. Save the program file, then compile and execute the program to see variable contents and dereferenced value

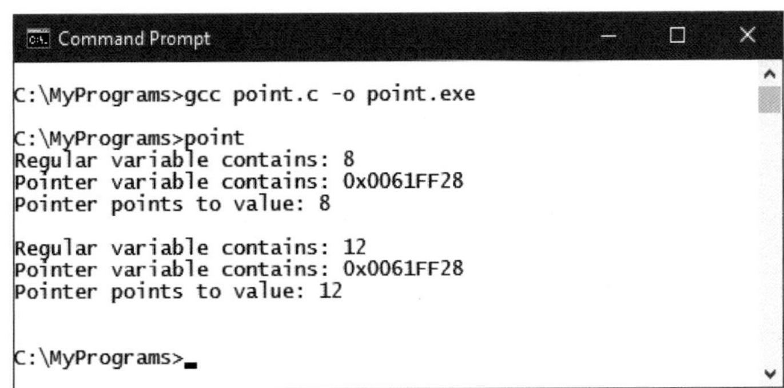

Command Prompt
C:\MyPrograms>gcc point.c -o point.exe
C:\MyPrograms>point
Regular variable contains: 8
Pointer variable contains: 0x0061FF28
Pointer points to value: 8
Regular variable contains: 12
Pointer variable contains: 0x0061FF28
Pointer points to value: 12
C:\MyPrograms>

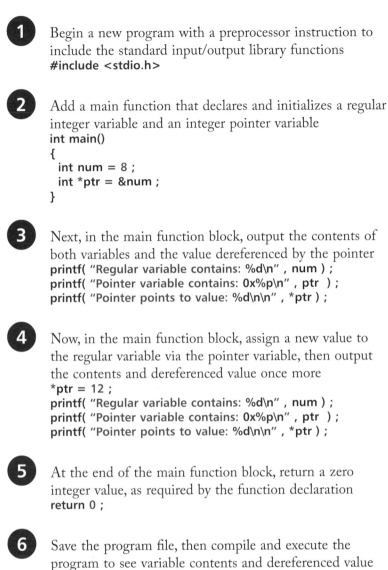

Declare variables before making other statements – for instance, at the beginning of **main()**.

Doing pointer arithmetic

Once a pointer has been created with an assigned memory address it can be reassigned another address, or moved using arithmetic.

The ++ increment operator and the -- decrement operator will move the pointer forward or back to other memory addresses for that data type – the larger the data type, the bigger the jump.

Even larger jumps can be achieved using the += and -= operators to specify how many places to jump.

Pointer arithmetic is especially useful with arrays because the elements in an array occupy consecutive memory places.

Assigning just the name of an array to a pointer automatically assigns it the memory address of the first element in that array. Incrementing the pointer by one then moves the pointer along to the next element's address.

movptr.c

The *= and /= operators cannot be used to move a pointer.

1. Begin a new program with a preprocessor instruction to include the standard input/output library functions

```
#include <stdio.h>
```

2. Add a main function that declares an integer variable, then declares and initializes an integer array variable

```
int main()
{
  int i ;
  int nums[10] = { 1, 2, 3, 4, 5, 6, 7, 8, 9, 10 } ;
}
```

3. Next, in the main function block, declare and initialize a pointer variable at the first array element, then output that address and the value dereferenced by that pointer

```
int *ptr = nums ;
printf( "\nAt Address: %p is Value: %d\n", ptr , *ptr ) ;
```

4. Now, in the main function block, increment the pointer to move along the array elements one by one

```
ptr++ ;
printf( "At Address: %p is Value: %d\n", ptr , *ptr ) ;
ptr++ ;
printf( "At Address: %p is Value: %d\n", ptr , *ptr ) ;
```

5. Now, jump back two memory places to the address of the first array element

```
ptr -= 2 ;
printf( "At Address: %p is Value: %d\n\n", ptr , *ptr ) ;
```

6. Next, add a loop to output each array element index number and the value it contains

```
for( i = 0 ; i < 10 ; i++ )
{
 printf( "Element %d Contains Value: %d\n" , i , *ptr ) ;
  ptr++ ;
}
```

7. At the end of the main function block, return a zero integer value, as required by the function declaration

```
return 0 ;
```

8. Save the program file, then compile and execute the program to see values output as the pointer moves between array elements

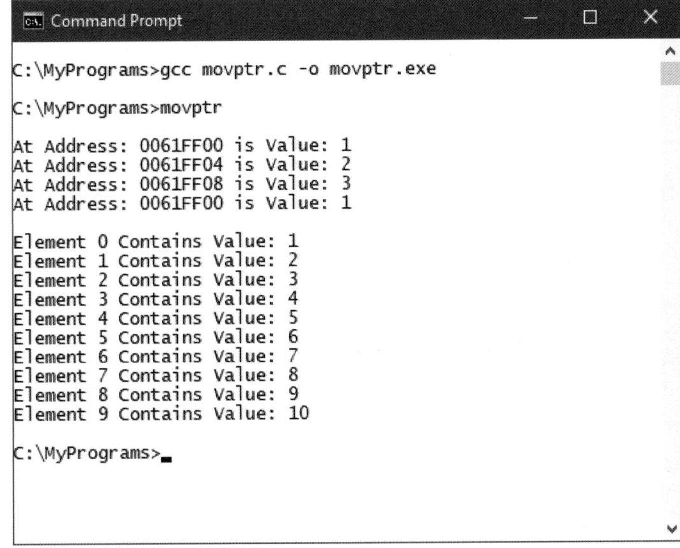

Command Prompt
C:\MyPrograms>gcc movptr.c -o movptr.exe
C:\MyPrograms>movptr
At Address: 0061FF00 is Value: 1
At Address: 0061FF04 is Value: 2
At Address: 0061FF08 is Value: 3
At Address: 0061FF00 is Value: 1
Element 0 Contains Value: 1
Element 1 Contains Value: 2
Element 2 Contains Value: 3
Element 3 Contains Value: 4
Element 4 Contains Value: 5
Element 5 Contains Value: 6
Element 6 Contains Value: 7
Element 7 Contains Value: 8
Element 8 Contains Value: 9
Element 9 Contains Value: 10
C:\MyPrograms>

The name of an array acts like a pointer to its first element.

Passing pointers to functions

In C programs, function arguments pass their data “by value” to a local variable inside the called function. This means that the function is not operating on the original value, but a copy of it.

Passing a pointer to the original value instead overcomes this to allow the called function to operate on the original value. This technique passes the data “by reference” and is a fundamental advantage provided by pointers.

passptr.c

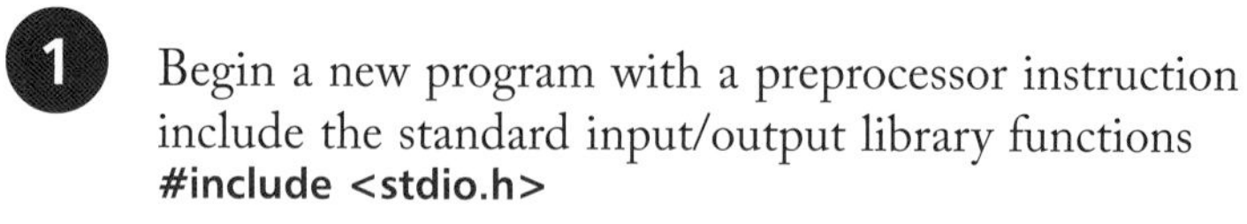

1. Begin a new program with a preprocessor instruction to include the standard input/output library functions

```
#include <stdio.h>
```

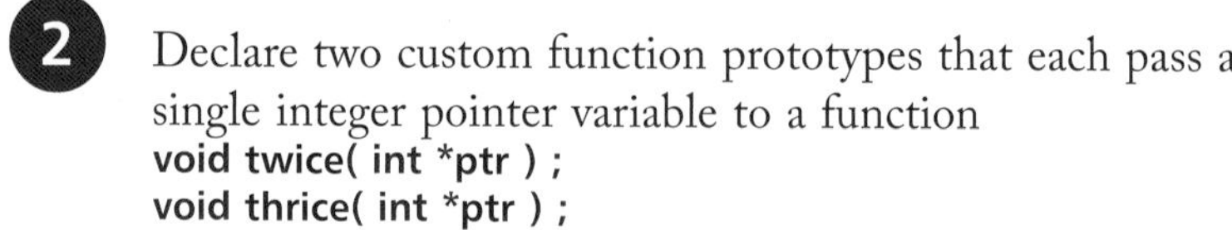

2. Declare two custom function prototypes that each pass a single integer pointer variable to a function

```
void twice( int *ptr ) ;
void thrice( int *ptr ) ;
```

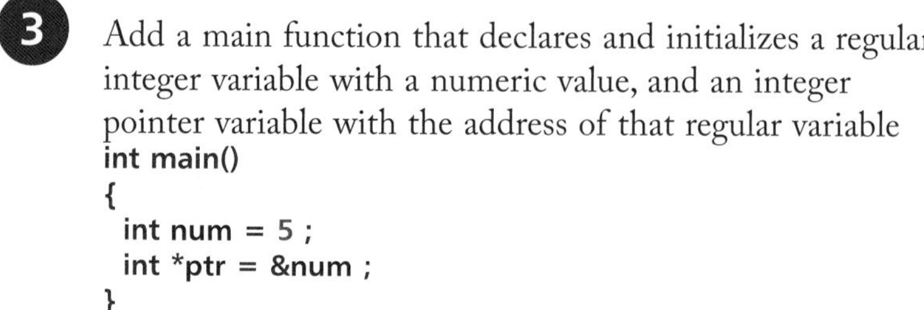

3. Add a main function that declares and initializes a regular integer variable with a numeric value, and an integer pointer variable with the address of that regular variable

```
int main()
{
  int num = 5 ;
  int *ptr = &num ;
}
```

4. Next, in the main function block, output the address stored by the pointer variable and the dereferenced value

```
printf( "ptr stores address: %p\n" , ptr ) ;
printf( "*ptr dereferences value: %d\n\n" , *ptr ) ;
```

5. Now, output the original value of the regular integer variable

```
printf( "The num value is %d\n" , num ) ;
```

Notice that the pointer argument must be included in the function prototype declaration.

6. After the main function block, define the two custom functions declared by the prototypes that each receive an integer pointer as an argument when called

```
void twice( int *number )
{
  *number = (*number * 2 ) ;
}

void thrice( int *number )
{
  *number = ( *number * 3 ) ;
}
```

The * character in the definition parentheses denotes that the argument is a pointer, whereas in the statement it dereferences the argument when it appears before the argument name, and represents the multiplication operator in the arithmetic statement.

7. Back in the main function block, add calls to each custom function, passing the address of the regular variable as a reference, and output the modified original value of the regular variable

```
twice( ptr ) ;
printf( "The num value is now %d\n", num ) ;
thrice( ptr ) ;
printf( "And now the num value is %d\n", num ) ;
```

8. At the end of the main function block, return a zero integer value, as required by the function declaration

```
return 0 ;
```

9. Save the program file, then compile and execute the program to see the values output after passing a reference

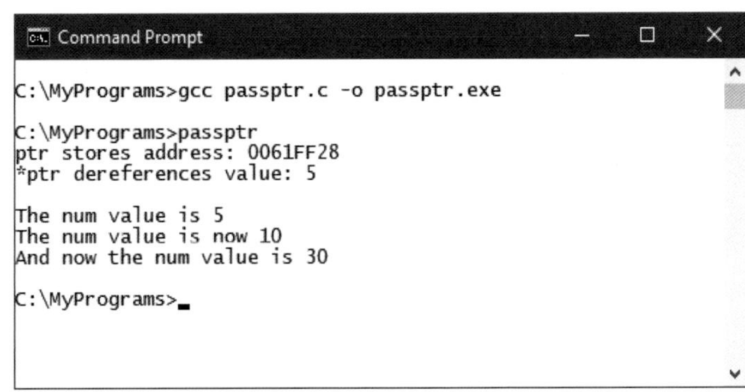

Command Prompt
C:\MyPrograms>gcc passptr.c -o passptr.exe
C:\MyPrograms>passptr
ptr stores address: 0061FF28
*ptr dereferences value: 5
The num value is 5
The num value is now 10
And now the num value is 30
C:\MyPrograms>

Creating arrays of pointers

A C program can contain arrays of pointers in which each element of an array stores the address of other variables.

This ability is especially useful for handling strings of characters. A character array that ends with the **\0** null character has string status, so can be assigned to a pointer variable. The name of a string **char** array acts like a pointer to its first element so the **&** addressof operator is not needed when assigning a string to a pointer variable.

arrptr.c

1. Begin a new program with a preprocessor instruction to include the standard input/output library functions

```
#include <stdio.h>
```

2. Add a main function that declares an integer variable, then declares and initializes an integer array variable

```
int main()
{
  int i ;
  int nums[5] = { 1, 2, 3, 4, 5 } ;
}
```

3. Next, in the main function block, declare and initialize integer pointer variables with the address of each element

```
int *ptr0 = &nums[0] ;
int *ptr1 = &nums[1] ;
int *ptr2 = &nums[2] ;
int *ptr3 = &nums[3] ;
int *ptr4 = &nums[4] ;
```

4. Now, declare and initialize an integer pointer array, with each element containing one of the integer pointers

```
int *ptrs[5] = { ptr0 , ptr1 , ptr2 , ptr3 , ptr4 } ;
```

5. Next, declare and initialize a character array; a pointer to that array; and a character pointer array with a string in each element

```
char str[9] = { 'C', ' ', 'i', 's', ' ', 'F', 'u', 'n', '\0' } ;
char *string = str ;
char *strings[3] = { "Alpha", "Bravo", "Charlie" } ;
```

Notice how the value of the counter **i** is substituted for the element index number on each iteration of the loop.

6. Add a loop to output the address of each integer pointer array element and their dereferenced values

```
for( i = 0 ; i < 5 ; i++ )
{
 printf( "The value at %p is: %d\n" , ptrs[i], *ptrs[i] ) ;
}
```

7. Add a statement to output the value stored in the character array

```
printf( "\nString is: %s\n\n" , string ) ;
```

8. Add a loop to output the string stored in each character pointer array element

```
for( i = 0 ; i < 3 ; i++ )
{
 printf( "String %d is: %s\n" , i , strings[i] ) ;
}
```

9. At the end of the main function block, return a zero integer value, as required by the function declaration

```
return 0 ;
```

10. Save the program file, then compile and execute the program to see the values output from the pointer array elements

```
Command Prompt

C:\MyPrograms>gcc arrptr.c -o arrptr.exe

C:\MyPrograms>arrptr
The value at 0061FF00 is: 1
The value at 0061FF04 is: 2
The value at 0061FF08 is: 3
The value at 0061FF0C is: 4
The value at 0061FF10 is: 5

String is: C is Fun

String 0 is: Alpha
String 1 is: Bravo
String 2 is: Charlie

C:\MyPrograms>_
```

The entire string in a **char** array is referenced by the pointer name alone – without the * dereference operator.

To include a space in a string there must actually be a space between the single quotes, like this ' ' – two single quotes together, such as '' is seen as an empty element and causes a compiler error.

Pointing to functions

Pointers can be created that point to functions, although this ability is used less than pointers that point to data values.

A pointer to a function is like a pointer to data but must always be enclosed within parentheses when using the * dereference operator to avoid a compiler error. These will also be followed by further parentheses containing any arguments to be passed to the function to which the pointer points.

The function pointer contains the address in memory at which the function to which it points begins. When the function pointer is dereferenced, the function to which it points gets called, and any arguments specified to the function pointer get passed to the called function.

A function pointer can even be passed as an argument to another function – so the receiving function may then call the function to which the function pointer points.

fcnptr.c

1. Begin a new program with a preprocessor instruction to include the standard input/output library functions

```
#include <stdio.h>
```

2. Declare a custom function prototype that has an integer argument, and another that has both a function pointer argument and an integer argument

```
int bounce( int a ) ;
int caller( int (*function) (int), int b ) ;
```

3. Add a main function that declares an integer variable, then declares and initializes a function pointer variable

```
int main()
{
  int  num ;
  int (*fptr)(int) = bounce ;
}
```

4. After the main function block, define the first custom function to output a received value and return an integer

```
int bounce( int a )
{
  printf( "\nReceived Value: %d\n", a ) ;
  return ( ( 3 * a ) + 3 ) ;
}
```

5 Next, define the second custom function to call a regular function from a received function pointer, and pass it a received integer value

```
int caller( int (*function)(int), int b )
{
  (*function)(b);
}
```

6 Back in the main function block, assign a value to the integer variable by calling the regular function via the function pointer, and output the value it returns

```
num = (*fptr)(10);
printf( "Returned Value: %d\n" , num ) ;
```

7 Now, assign a new value to the integer variable by passing the function pointer and an integer to another function, which in turn calls the regular function, then output the value it returns

```
num = caller( fptr, 5 ) ;
printf( "Returned Value: %d\n", num ) ;
```

8 At the end of the main function block, return a zero integer value, as required by the function declaration

```
return 0 ;
```

9 Save the program file, then compile and execute the program to see the values output via function pointers

```
Command Prompt
C:\MyPrograms>gcc fcnptr.c -o fcnptr.exe

C:\MyPrograms>fcnptr

Received Value: 10
Returned Value: 33

Received Value: 5
Returned Value: 18

C:\MyPrograms>_
```

The first argument to the **caller()** function in this example may be a pointer to any function that receives one integer argument and returns an integer value – as specified in the prototype declaration.

Like other pointers in C programming, a function pointer simply stores a memory address. When a function pointer is dereferenced with * the function at that address to which the pointer points gets called.

Summary

- A pointer is a variable that stores the memory address of another variable expressed in hexadecimal.
- The * dereference operator is used to reference the value contained in the variable to which the pointer points.
- In a pointer variable declaration, the variable name is prefixed by the * character to denote that the variable will be a pointer.
- A pointer variable can be assigned the address of another variable using the **&** addressof operator.
- Pointer arithmetic allows a pointer to move between consecutive memory places and is especially useful for moving between array elements.
- When an integer variable array name is assigned to a pointer, that pointer automatically stores the memory address of the first element of the array.
- Pointers can be passed as arguments to other functions.
- Passing a pointer as a function argument passes by reference, allowing that function to operate on the original value.
- Each element in an array of pointers can store the address of another variable.
- An array of pointers is especially useful for handling strings of characters.
- When a character string variable array name is assigned to a pointer, that pointer automatically stores the entire string.
- A pointer to a function must always be enclosed within parentheses when using the * dereference operator, to avoid compiler errors.
- Dereferencing a function pointer calls the function to which it points and passes any arguments specified to the pointer.

8 Manipulating Strings

This chapter demonstrates how strings of text may be manipulated in C programs.

110 Reading strings
112 Copying strings
114 Joining strings
116 Finding substrings
118 Validating strings
120 Converting strings
122 Summary

Reading strings

In C programming, a string is an array of characters that has the special **\0** null character in its last element. Each character, including punctuation and non-printing characters such as newline, has a unique numerical ASCII code value. This means that characters can be changed arithmetically. For example, where **char letter = 'S'** then **letter++** changes the value to **'T'**. ASCII code values for lowercase letters are always 32 higher than those of uppercase letters, so the case of any character can be changed by adding or subtracting a value of 32. For example, where **char letter = 'M'** then **letter+=32** changes the value to **'m'**. As C does not have a dedicated string data type, string variables must be created as character arrays, remembering to add a final element for the **\0** null character to promote the array to string constant status. This means that the name of an array then acts like an implied pointer to the entire string of characters. The **sizeof** operator will return the string's array length when the string name is supplied as its argument. A string may be assigned to an array or to a pointer of the **char** data type, like this:

You can find the standard ASCII character code table on pages 162-163.

```
char arr[6] = { 'A', 'l', 'p', 'h', 'a' } ;
char *ptr = "Beta" ;
printf( "%s" , arr ) ;      /* Outputs "Alpha"      */
printf( "%s" , ptr ) ;      /* Outputs "Beta"       */
```

In C, character values must be enclosed by single quotes, and strings must be enclosed by double quotes.

String values can be introduced into a C program by input from the user via the **scanf()** function described on page 24. This function works well for single characters or multiple characters forming a single word, but **scanf()** has a severe limitation in that it stops reading when it encounters a space. This means that the user cannot input a sentence via **scanf()** as the string gets truncated at the space following the first word. The solution to the **scanf()** problem is provided by two alternative functions located in the **stdio.h** header file. The first of these is named **fgets()** and can be used to read input from the user. This accepts all characters, including spaces, and assigns the string to a character array specified as its first argument. Its second argument must specify the number of characters to read, and its third argument must specify where to read from, such as **stdin** to read standard input. The **fgets()** function automatically adds the **\0** null character at the end of the string when the user hits the Return key – to ensure the input has string constant status. The companion to **fgets()** is the **puts()** function that will output a string specified as its argument and automatically add a newline character at the end.

fgetsputs.c

1. Begin a new program with a preprocessor instruction to include the standard input/output library functions

```
#include <stdio.h>
```

2. Add a main function that declares a character array

```
int main()
{
  char str[51] ;
}
```

3. Next, in the main function block, request input from the user and assign it to the array variable

```
printf( "\nEnter up to 50 characters with spaces:\n" ) ;
fgets( str , sizeof( str ), stdin ) ;
```

4. Now, in the main function block, output the string stored in the array variable

```
printf( "fgets() read: " ) ;
puts( str ) ;
```

5. Repeat the process to see the **scanf()** limitation

```
printf( "\nEnter up to 50 characters with spaces:\n" ) ;
scanf( "%s", str ) ;
printf( "scanf() read: %s\n" , str ) ;
```

6. At the end of the main function block, return a zero integer value, as required by the function declaration

```
return 0 ;
```

7. Save the program file, then compile and execute the program to see the string results

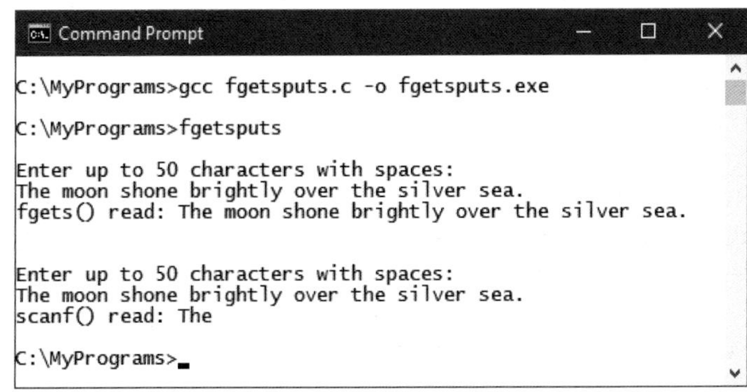

Command Prompt
C:\MyPrograms>gcc fgetsputs.c -o fgetsputs.exe
C:\MyPrograms>fgetsputs
Enter up to 50 characters with spaces:
The moon shone brightly over the silver sea.
fgets() read: The moon shone brightly over the silver sea.
Enter up to 50 characters with spaces:
The moon shone brightly over the silver sea.
scanf() read: The
C:\MyPrograms>

If you don't want a newline added after the output, use **printf()** instead of **puts()**.

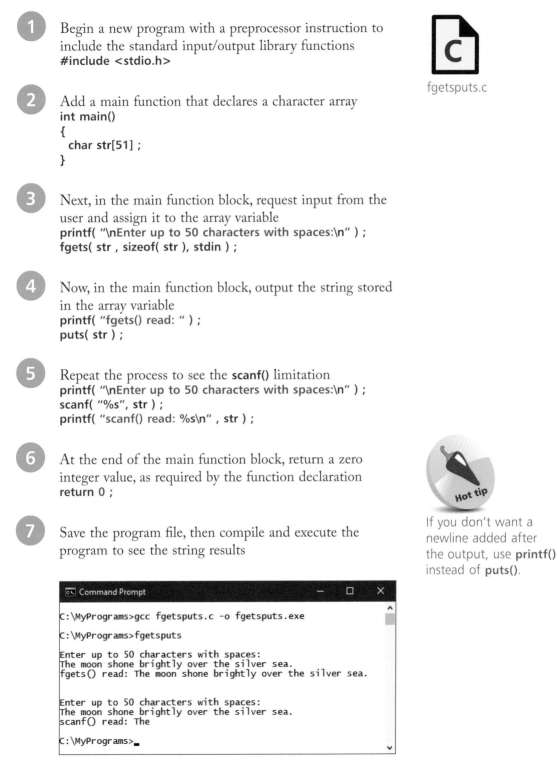

Copying strings

The standard C libraries include a header file named **string.h** that contains special string-handling functions. To make these available to a program the **string.h** header file must be added with an **#include** directive at the start of the program.

One of the functions in the **string.h** file is **strlen()**, which can be used to find the length of a string supplied as its argument. The **strlen()** function returns an integer that is the total number of characters in the string – including space "characters", but excluding the final **\0** null character.

Ensure that the target array is of sufficient size to hold all the characters of the string being copied – including a terminating **\0** null character.

The **string.h** header file also provides two useful functions to copy strings from one array to another. The first of these is **strcpy()**, which requires two arguments to be specified. The first argument specifies the name of the target array to copy the string into, and the second argument specifies the name of the source array from where the string should be copied. So, its syntax looks like this:

strcpy(***target-array*** **,** ***source-array*** **) ;**

All characters in the source array are copied into the target array, including the **\0** null terminating character. If there are other elements after the null character these are also padded with **\0**. This ensures that remnants from a longer original string are removed when a shorter string is copied into an array.

The second string-copying function is the similarly named **strncpy()** function (with an added "n"). This is used like the **strcpy()** function but takes a third argument to specify how much of the string to copy. Its syntax therefore looks like this:

strncpy(***target-array*** **,** ***source-array*** **,** ***length*** **) ;**

The string being copied will begin with the first character of the source array but will end at the position specified by the third argument – so the final **\0** null character is not automatically copied. After the characters have been copied, the next element in the target array must be assigned a terminating **\0** null character to promote the array to constant string status. Thus it is necessary to ensure that the target array is always one element larger than the actual number of characters being copied into it, including space "characters", to accommodate the final **\0** null character.

strcpy.c

1. Begin a new program with a preprocessor instruction to include the standard input/output and string functions
```
#include <stdio.h>
#include <string.h>
```

2. Add a main function that declares and initializes two character array variables with strings
```
int main()
{
  char s1[] = "Larger text string", s2[] = "Smaller string" ;
}
```

3. Next, in the main function block, output the first array contents together with its size and the string length
```
printf( "\n%s: %d elements" , s1 , sizeof(s1) ) ;
printf( ", %d characters\n" , strlen(s1) ) ;
```

4. Now, in the main function block, copy the entire contents of the second array into the first array
```
strcpy( s1, s2 ) ;
```

5. Repeat Step 3, to output the first array characteristics once more, then copy just the first five characters of the second array into the first array and add a null terminator
```
strncpy( s1, s2, 5 ) ;
s1[5] = '\0' ;
```

6. Repeat Step 3, to output the first array characteristics again, then finally return the required zero integer value
```
return 0 ;
```

7. Save the program file, then compile and execute the program to see the copied strings

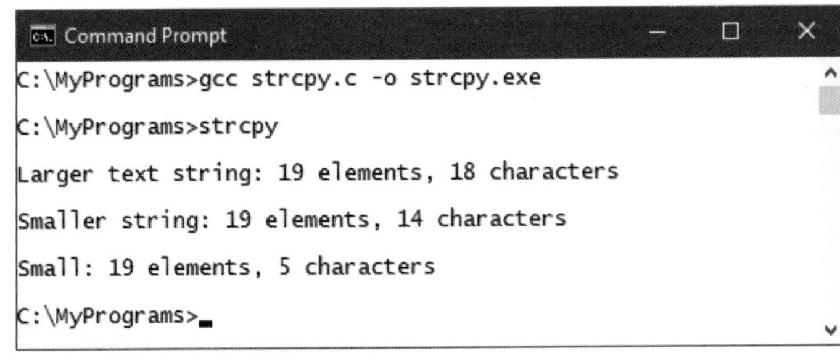

Command Prompt
C:\MyPrograms>gcc strcpy.c -o strcpy.exe
C:\MyPrograms>strcpy
Larger text string: 19 elements, 18 characters
Smaller string: 19 elements, 14 characters
Small: 19 elements, 5 characters
C:\MyPrograms>

Notice that the initial size of the arrays need not be specified in their declarations because the declarations also initialize them. Other arrays that are to be initialized later – say, by user input or by copying from another array – must specify a size in their declarations.

Here the sixth element in the final **s1** string is **s1[5]** – because array index numbering begins at zero, not one.

Joining strings

The combining of two strings into one single string is more precisely known as string "concatenation".

The standard C library **string.h** header file contains two functions that can be used to concatenate strings. To make these available to a program the **string.h** header file must be added with an **#include** directive at the start of the program.

The first string concatenation function is **strcat()**, which requires two arguments to be specified stating the names of the two strings to concatenate. The string named as its second argument is appended after the string named as its first argument, then the function returns the entire concatenated first string. So, the function's syntax looks like this:

strcat(***first-string* , *string-to-add-to-first-string*** **) ;**

It is important to note that the first string array must be large enough to accommodate all the characters of the concatenated strings to avoid an error.

The second string-concatenation function is the similarly named **strncat()** function (with an added "n"). This is used like the **strcat()** function but takes a third argument to specify how many characters of the second string should be appended onto the first string. Its syntax therefore looks like this:

strncat(***first-string* , *string-to-add-to-first-string* , *length*** **) ;**

The string being appended will begin with the first character of the string specified by the second argument by default, and end at the position specified by the third argument. But as the name of the string is an implied pointer to its first character, pointer arithmetic can be used to indicate a different position at which to begin appending, with this syntax:

strncat(first-string , (string-to-add-to-first-string+places) , length);

Once again, as with the **strcat()** function, it is important that the first string array must be large enough to accommodate all the characters of the concatenated strings to avoid an error when using the **strncat()** function.

These functions change the original string length as they add characters.

strcat.c

1. Begin a new program with a preprocessor instruction to include the standard input/output and string functions
```
#include <stdio.h>
#include <string.h>
```

2. Add a main function that declares and initializes four character array variables with strings
```
int main()
{
  char s1[100] = "A Place for Everything " ;
  char s2[] = "and Everything in its Place" ;
  char s3[100] = "The Truth is Rarely Pure " ;
  char s4[] = "and Never Simple. - Oscar Wilde" ;
}
```

3. Next, in the main function block, append the second string onto the first and output the concatenated string
```
strcat( s1, s2 ) ; printf( "\n%s\n" , s1 ) ;
```

4. Append the first 17 characters of the fourth string onto the third and output the concatenated string
```
strncat( s3, s4, 17 ) ; printf( "\n%s\n" , s3 ) ;
```

5. Append the last 14 characters of the fourth string onto the third and output the concatenated string
```
strncat( s3, ( s4 + 17 ) , 14 ) ; printf( "\n%s\n" , s3 ) ;
```

6. At the end of the main function block, return a zero integer value, as required by the function declaration
```
return 0 ;
```

7. Save the program file, then compile and execute the program to see the concatenated strings

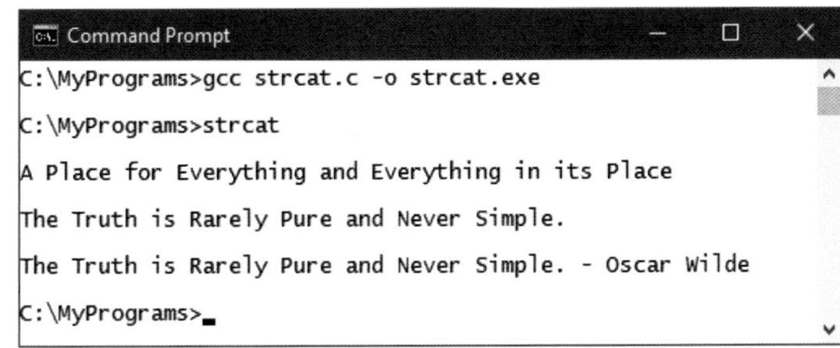

Command Prompt
C:\MyPrograms>gcc strcat.c -o strcat.exe
C:\MyPrograms>strcat
A Place for Everything and Everything in its Place
The Truth is Rarely Pure and Never Simple.
The Truth is Rarely Pure and Never Simple. - Oscar Wilde
C:\MyPrograms>

The string being lengthened must have an array size large enough to accommodate all characters of the combined strings.

Finding substrings

The **strstr()** function stops searching when it finds the first occurrence of a substring. Subsequent occurrences of that substring within the searched string will not be recognized.

A string can be searched to determine if it contains a specified "substring" sequence of characters with a function named **strstr()**. This is part of the standard library **string.h** header file, which must be added with an **#include** directive at the start of the program to make **strstr()** available.

The **strstr()** function takes two arguments – the first specifies the string to be searched, and the second specifies the substring to seek. If the substring is not found, the function returns a **NULL** value. When the substring is found, the function returns a pointer to the first character of the first occurrence of the substring.

The array index number of the element containing the first character of a located substring can be easily calculated using pointer arithmetic. Subtracting the address of the first character of the substring, returned by the **strstr()** function, from the address of the searched string's first character (to which the character array name points) can produce an integer value that is the index number of the first substring character within the searched string.

In C programming, the **==** and **!=** comparison operators can be used to compare a result against a **NULL** value but cannot be used to compare two strings. Instead, the **string.h** standard library header file provides a function named **strcmp()** for that purpose. This function takes two arguments that are the strings to be compared. The comparison is made based upon the numerical ASCII code value of each character and their position. When the strings are identical in every respect, including matching case, the **strcmp()** function returns zero. Otherwise, the function returns a positive or negative integer depending on the string values.

strstr.c

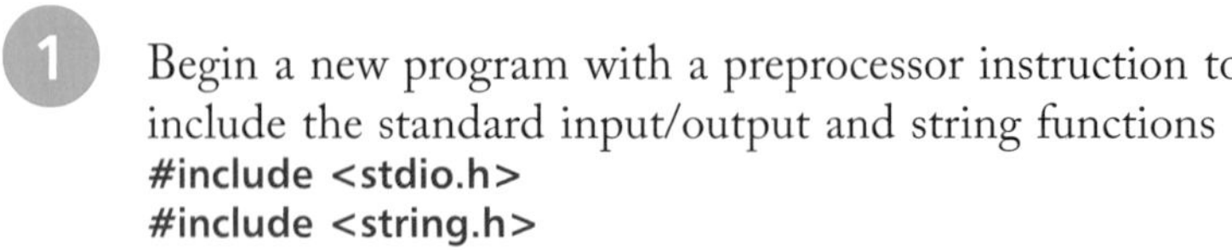

1. Begin a new program with a preprocessor instruction to include the standard input/output and string functions

```
#include <stdio.h>
#include <string.h>
```

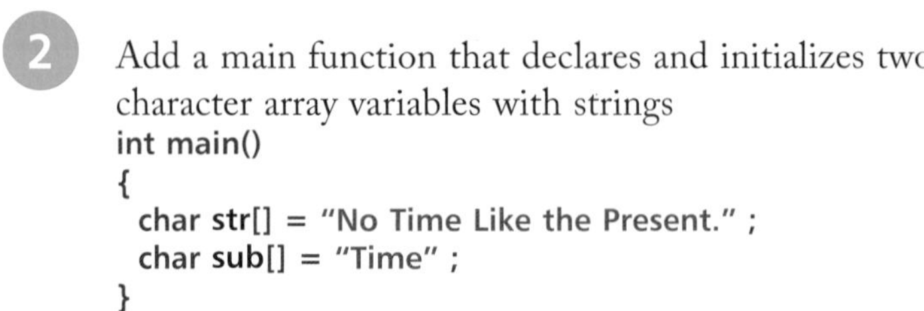

2. Add a main function that declares and initializes two character array variables with strings

```
int main()
{
  char str[] = "No Time Like the Present." ;
  char sub[] = "Time" ;
}
```

3. Next, in the main function block, output a message if the second string value cannot be found in the first string

```
if( strstr( str, sub ) == NULL )
{
  printf( "Substring \"Time\" Not Found\n" ) ;
}
```

4. Now, add statements to output the memory address and element index number within the first string at which the first character of the located substring occurs

```
else
{
  printf( "Substring \"Time\" Found at %p\n" , strstr( str, sub) ) ;
  printf( "Element Index Number %d\n\n", strstr(str,sub) - str ) ;
}
```

5. Output the result of three comparisons made against the value of the second string

```
printf("%s Versus \"Time\": %d\n",sub, strcmp(sub,"Time"));
printf("%s Versus \"time\": %d\n",sub, strcmp(sub,"time"));
printf("%s Versus \"TIME\": %d\n" ,sub, strcmp(sub,"TIME"));
```

6. At the end of the main function block, return a zero integer value, as required by the function declaration

```
return 0 ;
```

7. Save the program file, then compile and execute the program to see the result of searching for a substring and the comparison of three string values

```
Command Prompt

C:\MyPrograms>gcc strstr.c -o strstr.exe

C:\MyPrograms>strstr
Substring "Time" Found at 0061FF19
Element Index Number 3

Time Versus "Time": 0
Time Versus "time": -1
Time Versus "TIME": 1

C:\MyPrograms>_
```

Notice that the \ character in this example is used to escape the double-quote characters – to avoid premature termination of the output strings.

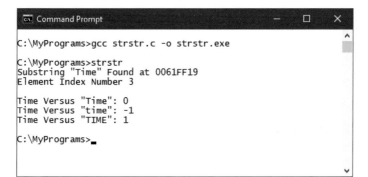

The **string.h** header file also contains two character-searching functions: **strchr()** finds the first occurrence of a character in a string, and **strrchr()** finds the last occurrence – both return **NULL** if the character is not found.

Validating strings

The standard library header file named **ctype.h** contains a number of functions that are useful to perform tests on characters. To make these available to a program, the **ctype.h** header file must be added with an **#include** directive at the start of the program.

Within the **ctype.h** header file, the **isalpha()** function tests whether a character is alphabetical, whereas **isdigit()** tests whether a character is numerical. Similarly, the **ispunct()** function tests whether a character is any other printable symbol, whereas the **isspace()** function tests whether a "character" is in fact a space.

Additionally, the **ctype.h** header provides **isupper()** and **islower()** functions to test the character case, along with **toupper()** and **tolower()** functions to change the character case.

Each test function returns a non-zero value (not necessarily a 1) when the tested character is as expected, but always returns a zero if it is not as expected.

These testing functions can be used to validate user string input by looping through characters in the string to examine each in turn. Where a character does not meet a required condition, a "flag" variable can be set to advise the user that the entry is invalid.

isval.c

1. Begin a new program with a preprocessor instruction to include the standard input/output and string functions

```
#include <stdio.h>
#include <string.h>
```

2. Add a main function that declares three variables, initializing a flag variable with a numeric true value (1)

```
int main()
{
  char str[7] ;
  int i ;
  int flag = 1 ;
}
```

3. Next, in the main function, request user input then assign that input as a string to the array variable

```
puts( "Enter six digits without any spaces..." ) ;
gets( str ) ;
```

4. Now, in the main function block, add a loop to examine each character in the array variable
   for(i = 0 ; i < 6 ; i++) {   }

The **isdigit()** test could alternatively be expressed like this: **isdigit() == 0**.

5. Within the loop block, change the flag variable to false (0) if any character is not a digit

```
if( !isdigit( str[i] ) )
{
  flag = 0 ;
}
```

6. Next, in the if block, describe any non-numeric character

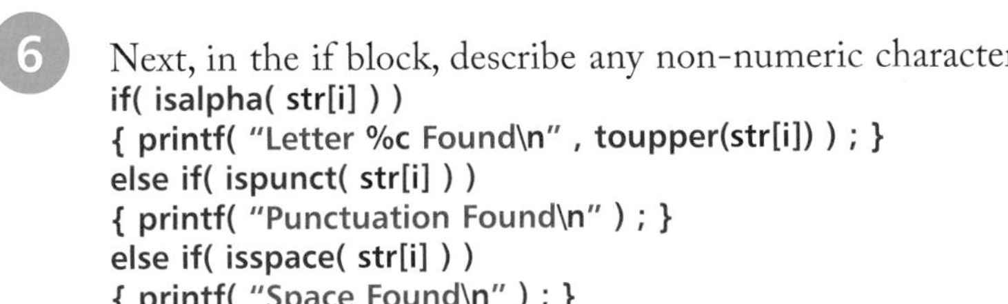

```
if( isalpha( str[i] ) )
{ printf( "Letter %c Found\n" , toupper(str[i]) ) ; }
else if( ispunct( str[i] ) )
{ printf( "Punctuation Found\n" ) ; }
else if( isspace( str[i] ) )
{ printf( "Space Found\n" ) ; }
```

7. After the loop block, output a message describing the flag variable state

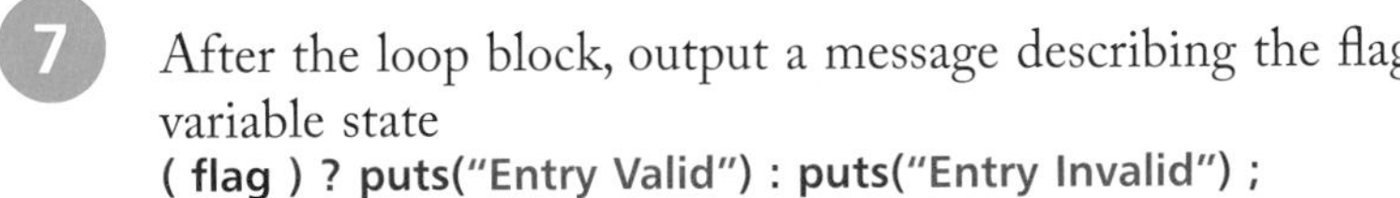

```
( flag ) ? puts("Entry Valid") : puts("Entry Invalid") ;
```


8. At the end of the main function block, return a zero integer value, as required by the function declaration
   return 0 ;

The full range of character test functions can be found in the Reference section on page 173.

9. Save the program file, then compile and execute the program to see validation of input strings

```
Command Prompt
C:\MyPrograms>gcc isval.c -o isval.exe

C:\MyPrograms>isval
Enter six digits without any spaces...
123456
Entry Valid

C:\MyPrograms>isval
Enter six digits without any spaces...
12345m
Letter M Found
Entry Invalid

C:\MyPrograms>isval
Enter six digits without any spaces...
1 3456
Space Found
Entry Invalid

C:\MyPrograms>_
```

Converting strings

The standard C library file **stdlib.h** contains a useful function named **atoi()** that can be used to convert a string to an integer. To make this function available to a program, the **stdlib.h** file must be added with an **#include** directive at the start of the program.

The **atoi()** function, alpha-to-integer, takes the string to be converted as its single argument. If the string is empty, or if the string's first character is not a number or a minus sign, then **atoi()** will return zero. Otherwise the string, or at least the numeric start of the string, will be converted to an int data type up until **atoi()** meets a non-numeric character in the string. When **atoi()** meets a non-numeric character in the string it returns the number so far converted as an **int** data type.

There is also an **itoa()** function, integer-to-alpha, that can be used to convert an **int** data type value to a string. This is widely used but is not part of the standard ANSI C specification. The **itoa()** function requires three arguments to specify the number to be converted; the string to which the converted number is to be assigned; and finally, the base to be used for the conversion. For example, a specified base of 2 will assign the binary equivalent of the specified numeric argument to the specified string argument.

An ANSI-compliant alternative to the **itoa()** function is the **sprintf()** function in the **stdlib.h** header file. It is less powerful because a base value cannot be specified. The **sprintf()** function also takes three arguments – the string to which the converted number is to be assigned, a format specifier, and the number to be converted. This function returns an integer that is the number of characters in the converted string.

conv.c

1. Begin a new program with a preprocessor instruction to include the standard input/output and conversion functions

```
#include <stdio.h>
#include <stdlib.h>
```

2. Add a main function that declares three integer variables, then declares and initializes three character arrays

```
int main()
{
  int n1, n2, n3 ;
  char s1[10]= "12eight", s2[10]= "-65.8", s3[10]= "x13" ;
}
```

3. Now, in the main function block, attempt to convert each string to an integer value and output the results

```
n1 = atoi( s1 ) ;
printf( "\nString %s converts to Integer: %d\n" , s1 , n1 ) ;

n2 = atoi( s2 ) ;
printf( "String %s converts to Integer: %d\n" , s2 , n2 ) ;

n3 = atoi( s3 ) ;
printf( "String %s converts to Integer: %d\n\n" , s3 , n3 ) ;
```

The **itoa()** function is very useful, but because it is not part of the ANSI standard it is not supported by all compilers – it is, however, supported by the GNU C Compiler featured in this book.

4. Next, in the function block, convert the first integer variable value to a string containing its binary equivalent using a non-standard function and output the result

```
itoa( n1, s1, 2 ) ;
printf( "Decimal %d is Binary: %s\n" , n1 , s1 ) ;
```

5. Then, convert the first integer variable value to strings containing its octal and hexadecimal equivalents using a standard library function and store their character length

```
n2 = sprintf( s3, "%o", n1 ) ;
printf( "Decimal %d is Octal: %s  chars: %d\n", n1, s3, n2) ;

n3 = sprintf( s3, "%x", n1 ) ;
printf("Decimal %d is Hexadecimal: %s  chars: %d\n",n1,s3,n3);
```

6. At the end of the main function block, return a zero integer value, as required by the function declaration

```
return 0 ;
```

Unlike the **itoa()** function, **sprintf()** cannot convert to binary because there is no format specifier for binary numbers.

7. Save the program file, then compile and execute the program to see the conversions

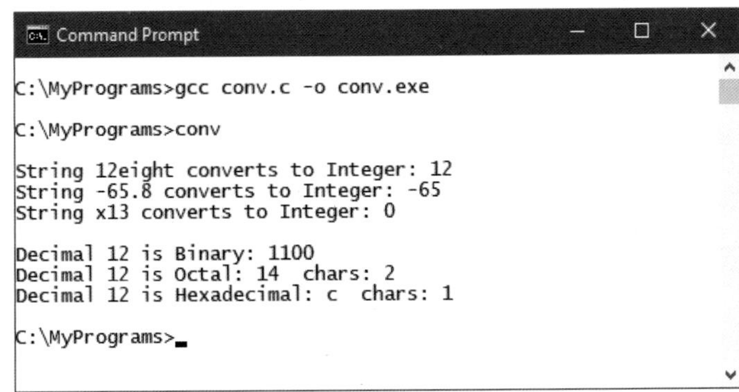

Command Prompt
C:\MyPrograms>gcc conv.c -o conv.exe
C:\MyPrograms>conv
String 12eight converts to Integer: 12
String -65.8 converts to Integer: -65
String x13 converts to Integer: 0
Decimal 12 is Binary: 1100
Decimal 12 is Octal: 14 chars: 2
Decimal 12 is Hexadecimal: c chars: 1
C:\MyPrograms>

Summary

- In C programming, a string is an array of characters that has the special **\0** null character in its final element.
- Each character also has a numerical ASCII code value.
- A character array name acts like a pointer to the entire string.
- The **scanf()** function stops reading input at the first space character it encounters, but the **gets()** function accepts spaces and automatically adds a final **\0** null character.
- The **puts()** function outputs a string specified as its argument and automatically adds a newline at the end of the string.
- Special string-handling functions are available from the standard C library **string.h** header file, such as the **strlen()** function that returns the length of a specified string, or the **strcpy()** and **strncpy()** functions that can copy strings.
- The **string.h** header file also provides the **strcat()** and **strncat()** functions, which can be used to concatenate strings together.
- Additionally, **string.h** provides the **strstr()** function that searches a string for a specified substring, and the **strcmp()** function that compares two specified strings.
- When **strstr()** fails to find the substring it seeks, the function returns a value of **NULL**.
- The standard C library **ctype.h** header file provides functions to test character types, such as **isalpha()**, **isdigit()** and **ispunc()**.
- The **ctype.h** header file also provides **islower()**, **isupper()** and **tolower()**, **toupper()** functions that test and set character case.
- The standard library **stdlib.h** header file provides the **atoi()** function that can convert a string to an integer.
- The standard library **stdlib.h** header file provides the **sprintf()** function that can convert an integer to a string, in much the same way as the more powerful non-standard **itoa()** function.

9 Building Structures

This chapter introduces the "struct" structure and "union" abstract data types, and demonstrates how they can be used in C programs to group together multiple variables of different types.

124 Grouping in a structure
126 Defining type structures
128 Using pointers in structures
130 Pointing to structures
132 Passing structures to functions
134 Grouping in a union
136 Allocating memory
138 Summary

Grouping in a structure

A structure in a C program can contain one or more variables of the same or different data types. These are grouped together in a single structure and can be conveniently referenced via its name. Variables within structures are known as its "members".

Grouping related variables together in a structure is helpful in organizing complicated data, especially in larger programs. For example, a structure could be created to describe a payroll record with variables to store an employee name, address, salary, tax, etc.

A structure is declared in a C program using the **struct** keyword followed by a given name and braces containing the variable members. Finally, the structure declaration must be terminated by a semi-colon after the closing brace; so a structure containing members to describe x and y coordinates of a point in a graph could look like this:

```
struct coords
{
  int x ;
  int y ;
} ;
```

Variable members of a structure cannot be immediately initialized in the struct declaration.

Optionally, "tag" names can be included just before the terminating semi-colon as a comma-separated list. In effect, the structure declaration defines a new data type, and tag names act like variables of that data type. For example, a variable named "point" of the data type "coords" can be declared like this:

```
struct coords
{
  int x ;
  int y ;
} point ;
```

Typically, a **struct** declaration will appear before the **main()** function in a C program.

Each **struct** member can then be referenced by appending the "." operator and the member name to the tag name, such as **point.x**.

Also, a new structure variable can be declared using the name of an existing structure, and that new variable will inherit the original member properties. For example, create a new structure variable named "top" based on the structure named "coords" with members **top.x** and **top.y** with this declaration:

```
struct coords top ;
```

struct.c

1. Begin a new program with a preprocessor instruction to include the standard input/output library functions
```
#include <stdio.h>
```

2. Declare a structure with two members and one tag
```
struct coords
{
  int x ;
  int y ;
} point ;
```

3. Then, create another instance of the structure
```
struct coords top ;
```

4. Next, add a main function that initializes both members of each structure
```
int main()
{
  point.x = 5 ; point.y = 8 ;
  top.x = 15 ; top.y = 24 ;
}
```

5. Now, output the value stored in each structure member
```
printf( "\npoint x: %d, point y: %d\n", point.x , point.y ) ;
printf( "\ntop x: %d, top y: %d\n" , top.x , top.y ) ;
```

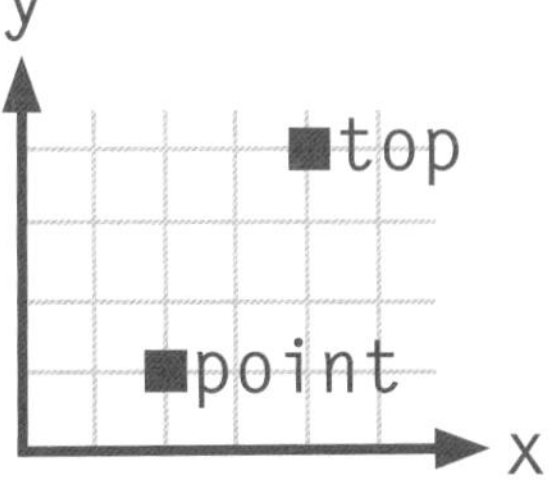

6. At the end of the main function block, return a zero integer value, as required by the function declaration
```
return 0 ;
```

7. Save the program file, then compile and execute the program to see the values stored in structure members

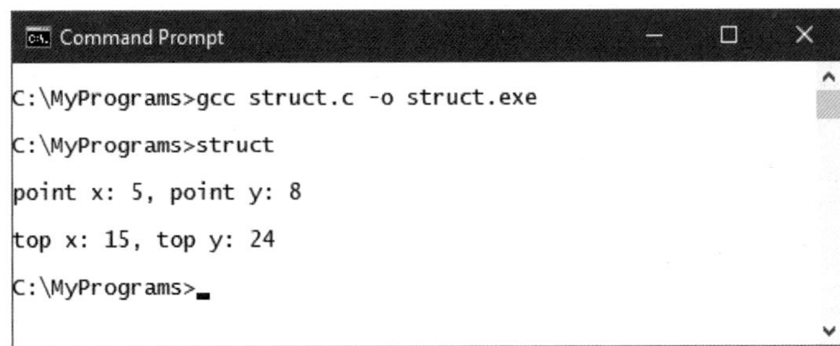
```
Command Prompt
C:\MyPrograms>gcc struct.c -o struct.exe

C:\MyPrograms>struct

point x: 5, point y: 8

top x: 15, top y: 24

C:\MyPrograms>
```

Defining type structures

A data type defined by a structure can be declared to be an actual data type definition by adding the **typedef** keyword at the very beginning of the structure declaration. This identifies the structure to be a prototype from which other structures can be declared simply using any of its tag names – without the **struct** keyword.

Using **typedef** may often help simplify the code by not requiring the **struct** keyword when declaring variables of a data type defined in a structure. It is helpful, however, to capitalize the tag name so it is easily recognizable as a structure-defined data type.

Declarations of variables of data types defined in a structure may optionally initialize all their members by assigning values as a comma-separated list within braces.

Structures may also be nested within other structures. In that case, individual members are referenced using two "." dot operators, with the syntax ***outer-structure.inner-structure.member***.

typedef.c

1. Begin a new program with a preprocessor instruction to include the standard input/output library functions

```
#include <stdio.h>
```

2. Declare an un-named structure defining a data type with two members and one tag

```
typedef struct
{
  int x ;
  int y ;
} Point ;
```

3. Then, create two variables of the structure-defined data type, initializing both members of one variable

```
Point top = { 15 , 24 } ;
Point btm ;
```

4. Next, add a main function that initializes both members of the other variable of the structure-defined data type

```
int main()
{
  btm.x = 5 ;
  btm.y = 8 ;
}
```

5 Now, output the coordinates of both points

```
printf( "\nTop x: %d, y: %d\n" , top.x , top.y ) ;
printf( "Bottom x: %d, y: %d\n" , btm.x , btm.y ) ;
```

6 Before the main function block, insert a second structure defining a data type with two nested structure members

```
typedef struct
{
  Point a ;
  Point b ;
} Box ;
```

Notice that the structure itself need not be named, as it is the tag name that's important.

7 Next, declare a variable of the second structure-defined data type, initializing all its members

```
Box rect = { 6 , 12 , 30 , 20 } ;
```

8 Back in the main function block, output the coordinates of all points contained in the nested structure members

```
printf( "\nPoint a x: %d" , rect.a.x ) ;
printf( "\nPoint a y: %d" , rect.a.y ) ;
printf( "\nPoint b x: %d" , rect.b.x ) ;
printf( "\nPoint b y: %d\n" , rect.b.y ) ;
```


9 At the end of the main function block, return a zero integer value, as required by the function declaration

```
return 0 ;
```

Struct members can only be initialized using a comma-separated list in the variable declaration – they must be individually initialized later.

10 Save the program file, then compile and execute the program to see the values stored in structure members

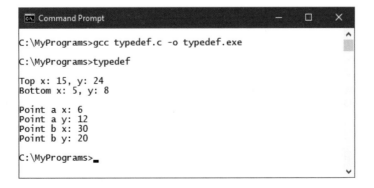

```
Command Prompt

C:\MyPrograms>gcc typedef.c -o typedef.exe

C:\MyPrograms>typedef

Top x: 15, y: 24
Bottom x: 5, y: 8

Point a x: 6
Point a y: 12
Point b x: 30
Point b y: 20

C:\MyPrograms>
```

Using pointers in structures

There is an advantage in using a character pointer in a structure as a string container over using a character array for the same purpose.

L-values are objects whereas R-values are data.

An entire string can only be assigned to a **char** array upon its declaration. The only way to subsequently assign a string to a **struct char** array using the = operator is to assign individual characters to one element at a time.

In each assignation the value to the left of the = operator is known as the "L-value", representing the memory Location, whereas the value to the right of the = operator is known as the "R-value", representing the data to Read into that location.

One important rule in C programming is that an R-value cannot appear on the left side of an = operator. An L-value, on the other hand, may appear on either side of an = operator.

Each individual element of a **char** array is an L-value to which an individual character may be assigned, but a **char** pointer is also an L-value to which an entire string may be assigned after that pointer has been declared.

strmbr.c

1. Begin a new program with a preprocessor instruction to include the standard input/output library functions

```
#include <stdio.h>
```

2. Next, declare an un-named structure defining a data type with a single character array member and one tag name

```
typedef struct
{
  char str[5] ;
} ArrType ;
```

3. Now, declare an un-named structure defining a data type with a single character pointer member and one tag name

```
typedef struct
{
  char *str ;
} PtrType ;
```

4. Then, declare one variable of each structure-defined data type, initializing the single member of each variable

```
ArrType arr = { 'B', 'a', 'd', ' ', '\0' } ;
PtrType ptr = { "Good" } ;
```

5. Next, add a main function that outputs the string value of the variable character array member

```
int main()
{
  printf( "\nArray string is a %s" , arr.str ) ;
}
```

Notice that the members of different structures can be named alike without conflict.

6. Within the main function block, tediously assign new values to each element of the character array and output the new string value

```
arr.str[0] = 'I' ;
arr.str[1] = 'd' ;
arr.str[2] = 'e' ;
arr.str[3] = 'a' ;
arr.str[4] = '\0' ;
printf(  "%s\n" , arr.str ) ;
```

7. Next, output the string value of the variable character pointer member

```
printf( "\nPointer string is a %s" , ptr.str ) ;
```

8. Now, easily assign a new value to the character pointer and output the new string value

```
ptr.str = "Idea" ;
printf( "%s\n" , ptr.str ) ;
```

The elements of a **char** array can only be initialized using a comma-separated list in its declaration.

9. At the end of the main function block, return a zero integer value, as required by the function declaration

```
return 0 ;
```

10. Save the program file, then compile and execute the program to see the values stored in the structure members

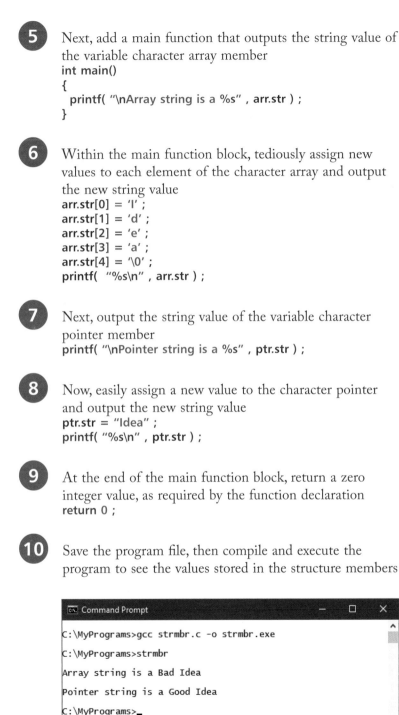

```
Command Prompt
C:\MyPrograms>gcc strmbr.c -o strmbr.exe

C:\MyPrograms>strmbr

Array string is a Bad Idea

Pointer string is a Good Idea

C:\MyPrograms>_
```

Pointing to structures

Pointers to struct data types can be created in just the same way as pointers to regular data types. In this case, the pointer holds the address of the beginning of the region of memory used to store the member data.

The use of pointers to structures is so common in C programs that there is even a special operator to describe it. In a struct pointer the "." dot operator can be replaced by "->", which is a hyphen followed by the greater-than operator. This combination is known as the arrow operator. For example, a pointer to a struct member **ptr->member** is the equivalent of **(*ptr).member**.

structptr.c

1. Begin a new program with a preprocessor instruction to include the standard input/output library functions

```
#include <stdio.h>
```

2. Next, declare an un-named structure defining a data type with two character pointer members and one tag name

```
typedef struct
{
  char *name;  char *popn ;
} City ;
```

3. Now, add a main function that declares three regular variables and a pointer variable, all of the struct data type

```
int main()
{
  City ny , la , ch , *ptr ;
}
```

4. Within the main function block, assign values to members of the first variable then display the stored values, using the dot operator to both store and retrieve the values

```
ny.name = "New York City" ;
ny.popn = "8,274,527" ;
printf( "\n%s , Population: %s\n", ny.name , ny.popn ) ;
```

5. Assign the address of the second variable to the pointer variable

```
ptr = &la ;
```

The arrow operator is useful in C programming to differentiate between structure pointers and other pointers.

6 Now, assign values to members of the second variable, then display the stored values, using the arrow operator to store the values and the dot operator to retrieve the values

```
ptr->name = "Los Angeles" ;
ptr->popn = "3,834,340" ;
printf( "\n%s, Population: %s\n" , la.name, la.popn ) ;
```

The population values in this example are assigned as strings to preserve the comma separations.

7 Next, assign the address of the third variable to the pointer variable

```
ptr = &ch ;
```

8 Now, assign values to members of the third variable, then display the stored values, using the arrow operator to both store and retrieve the values

```
ptr->name = "Chicago" ;
ptr->popn = "2,836,658" ;
printf( "\n%s, Population: %s\n", ptr->name, ptr->popn ) ;
```

9 At the end of the main function block, return a zero integer value, as required by the function declaration

```
return 0 ;
```

10 Save the program file, then compile and execute the program to see the values stored in the structure members

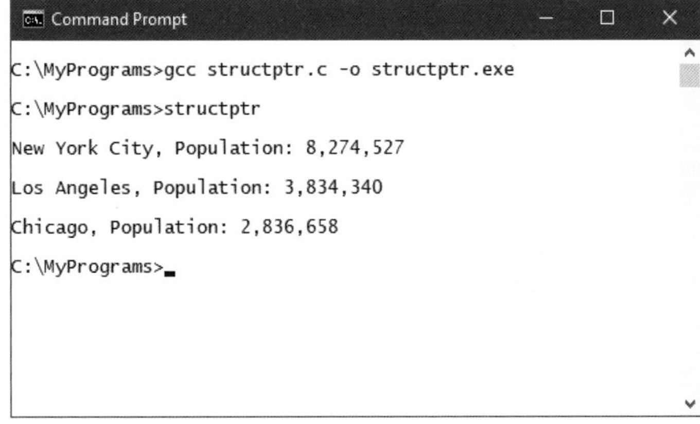

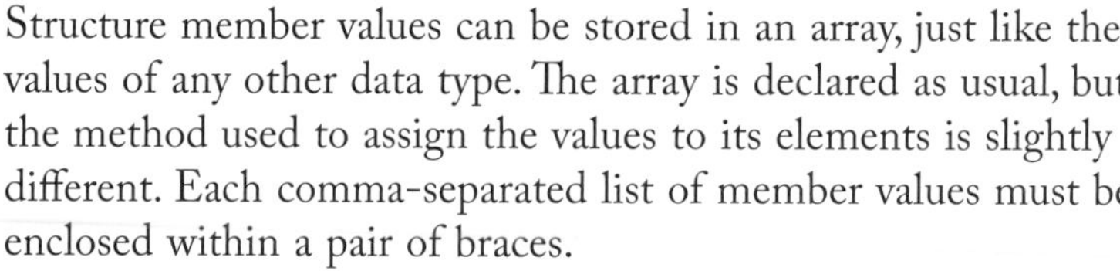

Passing structures to functions

Structure member values can be stored in an array, just like the values of any other data type. The array is declared as usual, but the method used to assign the values to its elements is slightly different. Each comma-separated list of member values must be enclosed within a pair of braces.

Similarly, a **struct** can be passed as an argument to a function, just like any other variable. The structure's data type must be specified in both the function prototype declaration and its definition, along with a variable name by which the function can address its member values.

But remember that passing by value, simply using a regular variable, means that the function will operate on a copy of the struct – its original member values will remain unchanged. Passing the struct by reference, on the other hand, using a pointer variable, means that the function will operate on the original **struct** members – so the original member values will get changed.

Beware

Simply assigning all the values as a comma-separated list will not work – each set of values must be enclosed by its own pair of braces.

passstruct.c

1. Begin a new program with a preprocessor instruction to include the standard input/output library functions

```
#include <stdio.h>
```

2. Next, declare an un-named structure defining a data type with two members and one tag name

```
typedef struct
{
  char *name ;
  int quantity ;
} Item ;
```

3. Now, declare an array of the structure's data type, initializing each member of three structures

```
Item fruits[3] =
      { { "Apple" , 10 }, { "Orange" , 20 }, { "Pear" , 30 } } ;
```

4. Add a function prototype that will pass a structure variable and a pointer variable to a structure as arguments

```
void display( Item val , Item *ref ) ;
```

5. Now, define the function declared in the prototype that begins by revealing the value of the passed arguments
```
void display( Item val , Item *ref  )
{ printf( "%s: %d\n" , val.name , val.quantity ) ; }
```

6. Next, in the function block, change the values of the struct member copies passed then output the new values
```
val.name = "Banana" ; val.quantity = 40 ;
printf( "%s: %d\n" , val.name , val.quantity ) ;
```

7. Confirm that the original values are unchanged
```
printf( "%s: %d\n" , fruits[0].name , fruits[0].quantity ) ;
```

8. Then, change the original member values and output the new values
```
ref->name = "Peach" ;
ref->quantity = 50 ;
printf( "%s: %d\n" , fruits[0].name , fruits[0].quantity ) ;
```

9. Just before the function block, insert a main function that calls the other function, passing a struct and a pointer as arguments
```
int main()
{
  display( fruits[0] , &fruits[0] ) ;
}
```

10. At the end of the main function block, return a zero integer value, as required by the function declaration
```
return 0 ;
```

11. Save the program file, then compile and execute the program to see the values stored in the structure members

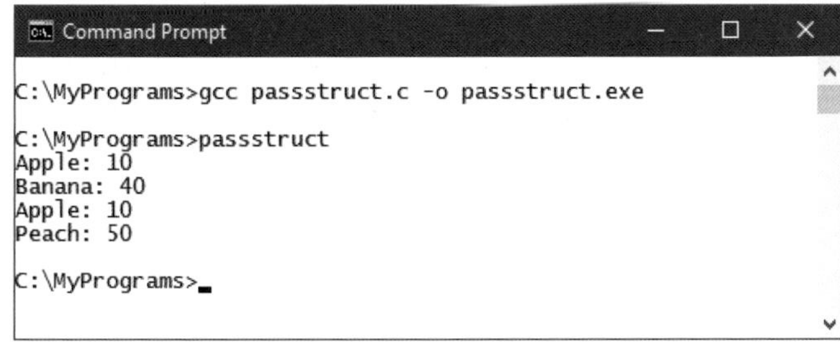
```
C:\MyPrograms>gcc passstruct.c -o passstruct.exe

C:\MyPrograms>passstruct
Apple: 10
Banana: 40
Apple: 10
Peach: 50

C:\MyPrograms>_
```

Passing large structs by value is inefficient as it creates a copy of the entire struct in memory, whereas passing by reference only requires the size of a pointer.

Grouping in a union

In C programming, a "union" allows different pieces of data, of any data type, to be stored at the same memory location as the program proceeds – assigning a value to the union will overwrite that previously stored there. This allows efficient use of memory.

A union is like a **struct** but is declared with the **union** keyword and, because of its nature, its members can only be assigned values individually as the program proceeds.

An array of unions can be created in the same way as an array of structs was created in the previous example, but **union** members can only be initialized in the declaration if they are all of the same data type. A pointer to a **union** can be created in exactly the same manner in which a pointer to a **struct** is created and a **union** can be passed to a function just like any other variable.

1. Begin a new program with a preprocessor instruction to include the standard input/output library functions
```
#include <stdio.h>
```

2. Next, declare an un-named structure defining a data type with three members and one tag name
```
typedef struct
{  int num ; char ltr, *str ; }  Distinct ;
```

3. Now, declare an un-named union defining a data type with three members and one tag name
```
typedef union { int num ; char ltr , *str ; }  Unified ;
```

4. Add a main function that declares a variable of the struct's data type and initializes each of its members
```
int main()
{
  Distinct sdata = { 10 , 'C' , "Program" } ;
}
```

5. Now, in the main function block, declare a variable of the union data type
```
Unified udata ;
```

It is the programmer's responsibility to understand which type of data is being stored in a union at any point in the execution of a program.

6 After the variable declarations, output the value and memory address of each struct member

```
printf( "\nStructure:\nNumber: %d", sdata.num ) ;
printf( "\tStored at: %p\n" , &sdata.num ) ;
printf( "Letter: %c" , sdata.ltr ) ;
printf( "\tStored at: %p\n" , &sdata.ltr ) ;
printf( "String: %s" , sdata.str ) ;
printf( "\tStored at: %p\n" , &sdata.str ) ;
```

Hot tip

Unions are mostly useful when memory is very limited.

7 Now, assign a value to the first union member then output its value and memory address

```
udata.num = 16 ;
printf( "\nUnion:\nNumber: %d" , udata.num ) ;
printf( "\tStored at: %p\n" , &udata.num ) ;
```

8 Next, assign a value to the second union member then output its value and memory address

```
udata.ltr = 'A' ;
printf( "Letter: %c" , udata.ltr ) ;
printf( "\tStored at: %p\n" , &udata.ltr ) ;
```

9 Finally, assign a value to the third union member then output its value and memory address

```
udata.str = "Union" ;
printf( "String: %s", udata.str ) ;
printf( "\tStored at: %p\n" , &udata.str ) ;
```

10 At the end of the main function block, return a zero integer value, as required by the function declaration

```
return 0 ;
```

11 Save the program file, then compile and execute the program to see the values stored in the structure, and union members and the addresses where they are stored

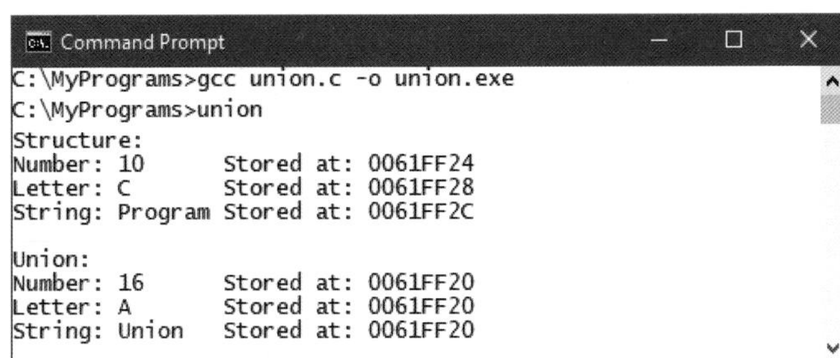
Command Prompt
C:\MyPrograms>gcc union.c -o union.exe
C:\MyPrograms>union
Structure:
Number: 10   Stored at: 0061FF24
Letter: C   Stored at: 0061FF28
String: Program Stored at: 0061FF2C
Union:
Number: 16   Stored at: 0061FF20
Letter: A   Stored at: 0061FF20
String: Union   Stored at: 0061FF20

Allocating memory

The standard C **stdlib.h** library header file provides memory management functions, with which a program can explicitly request memory be made available as the program executes. The **malloc()** function requires a single integer argument to specify how many bytes of memory to allocate, whereas the **calloc()** function requires two integer arguments that get multiplied together to specify how many bytes of memory to allocate. Both of these functions return a pointer to the beginning of the memory block when successful, or a **NULL** value upon failure.

The **calloc()** function clears all allocated memory space to zero, but **malloc()** leaves whatever values are already there.

Memory previously allocated with **malloc()** or **calloc()** can be increased with the **realloc()** function. This requires the pointer to the allocated memory block as its first argument, and an integer specifying the new block size as its second argument. It returns a pointer to the beginning of the enlarged memory block when successful, or a **NULL** value upon failure.

All memory allocated with these functions should be released when no longer required by specifying the memory block pointer as the argument to the **free()** function.

There is no standard C function to determine the size of a dynamically allocated memory block but this can be discovered with platform-specific functions. On Windows there is **_msize()** and on Linux there is **malloc_usable_size()**. Both these functions require the memory block pointer as their argument.

memory.c

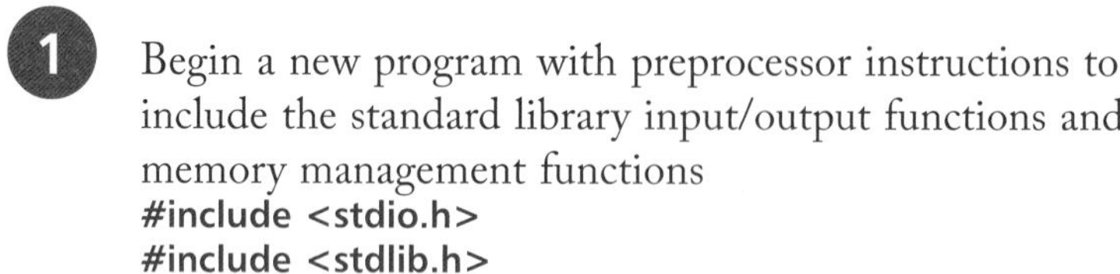

1. Begin a new program with preprocessor instructions to include the standard library input/output functions and memory management functions

```
#include <stdio.h>
#include <stdlib.h>
```

2. Declare a Windows-specific function prototype

```
int _msize( int *bytes ) ;
```

3. Add a main function that declares an integer variable and an integer pointer variable

```
int main()
{
  int size , *mem ;
}
```

On Linux systems, replace the **_msize** prototype declaration and function calls with the alternative **malloc_usable_size**.

4. Request memory to accommodate 100 integers

```
mem = malloc( 100 * sizeof( int ) ) ;
```

Even though an **int** typically occupies 4 bytes it is good practice to use the **sizeof()** operator to specify the size in case of variation.

5. Next, output details of the allocated memory block or an advisory message if the request fails

```
if( mem != NULL )
{
  size = _msize( mem ) ;
  printf( "\nSize of block for 100 ints: %d bytes\n", size ) ;
  printf( "Beginning at %p\n" , mem ) ;
}
else { printf( "!!! Insufficient memory\n") ; return 1 ; }
```

6. Now, attempt to enlarge the allocated memory block and output its details or an advisory message if the request fails

```
mem = realloc( mem , size + ( 100 * sizeof( int ) ) ) ;
if( mem != NULL )
{
  size = _msize( mem ) ;
  printf( "\nSize of block for 200 ints: %d bytes\n" , size ) ;
  printf( "Beginning at %p\n" , mem ) ;
}
else { printf( "!!! Insufficient memory\n") ; return 1 ; }
```

The implementation of the **realloc()** function can vary on different platforms.

7. At the end of the main function block, remember to release the allocated memory, then return the require zero integer value

```
free( mem ) ;
return 0 ;
```

8. Save the program file, then compile and execute the program to see the allocated memory blocks when the requests are successful

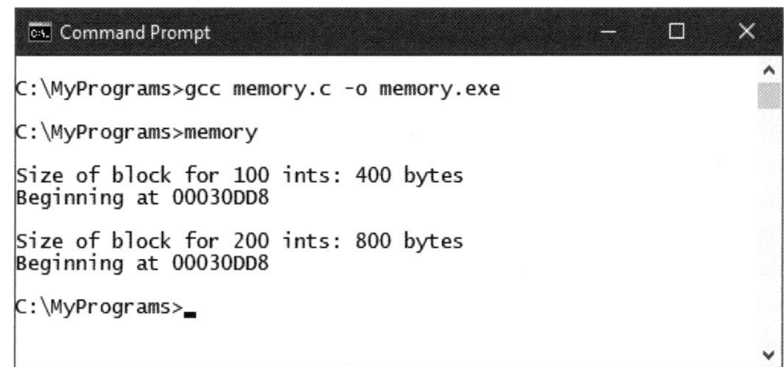

Command Prompt
C:\MyPrograms>gcc memory.c -o memory.exe
C:\MyPrograms>memory
Size of block for 100 ints: 400 bytes
Beginning at 00030DD8
Size of block for 200 ints: 800 bytes
Beginning at 00030DD8
C:\MyPrograms>

The memory request statement could alternatively have used **calloc(100 , sizeof(int))** .

Summary

- A **struct** can contain one or more variables of any data type, which are known as **struct** members.
- Each **struct** member can be referenced by appending its name to a tag name with the . dot operator.
- Further instances of a **struct** will inherit the member properties of the original from which they are derived.
- The **struct** keyword may be preceded by the **typedef** keyword to declare the struct to be a data type.
- It is helpful to capitalize tag names to readily identify structure-defined data types.
- Variable declarations may optionally initialize each **struct** member by assigning a comma-separated list of values.
- A pointer to a **struct** holds the memory address of the beginning of the region of memory used to store member data.
- In a struct pointer, the . dot operator can be replaced by the -> arrow operator.
- The members in an array of structures may, optionally, be initialized in the declaration – but each list of member values must be enclosed within a pair of braces.
- A **struct** may be passed as an argument to a function, just like any other variable.
- Passing a **struct** variable to a function means it will operate on a copy of the **struct** members, but passing a **struct** pointer variable means the function operates on the original members.
- A **union** is like a **struct** in which different pieces of data are stored at the same memory location as the program proceeds.
- The standard C library **stdlib.h** header file provides the **malloc()**, **calloc()** and **realloc()** functions, which can allocate memory, and the **free()** function to release allocated memory.

10 Producing Results

This chapter demonstrates how C programs can utilize files, system time, random numbers, and a simple Windows dialog box.

140 Creating a file
142 Reading & writing characters
144 Reading & writing lines
146 Reading & writing entire files
148 Scanning filestreams
150 Reporting errors
152 Getting the date and time
154 Running a timer
156 Generating random numbers
158 Displaying a dialog box
160 Summary

Creating a file

A special data type for handling files is defined in the **stdio.h** header file. It is called a "file pointer" and has the syntax **FILE *fp**. File pointers are used to open, read, write, and close files. In a C program, a file pointer called "file_ptr" can be created with the declaration **FILE *file_ptr ;** .

A file pointer points to a structure defined in the **stdio.h** header file that contains information about the file. This includes details about the current character and if the file is being read or written.

Before a file can be read or written it firstly must always be opened with the **fopen()** function. This takes two arguments to specify the name and location of the file, and a "mode" in which to open the file. The **fopen()** function returns a file pointer if successful, or a **NULL** value upon failure.

Once a file has been successfully opened it can be read or added to, or new text can be written in the file, depending on the mode specified in the call to the **fopen()** function. Following this, the open file must then always be closed by calling the **fclose()** function and specifying the file pointer as its single argument.

The table below lists all the possible file modes that can be specified as the second argument to the **fopen()** function:

File mode:	Operation:
r	Open an existing file to read
w	Open an existing file to write. Creates a new file if none exists, or opens an existing file and discards all its previous contents
a	Appends text. Opens or creates a text file for writing at the end of the file
r+	Opens a text file to read from or write to
w+	Opens a text file to write to or read from
a+	Opens or creates a text file to read from or write to at the end of the file

Note: Where the mode includes a **b** after any of the file modes listed above, the operation relates to a binary file rather than a text file – for example, **rb** or **w+b**

All the standard functions for file input/output are contained in the **stdio.h** header file.

For convenience, all the text files in the examples in this chapter are located in the **MyPrograms** folder that also contains the C source code files. On Windows the directory is **C:\MyPrograms**, and on Linux systems it's at **/home/MyPrograms**.

1. Begin a new program with a preprocessor instruction to include the standard input/output library functions

```
#include <stdio.h>
```

C

newfile.c

2. Add a main function that declares a file pointer

```
int main()
{
  FILE *file_ptr ;
}
```

3. Next, in the main function block, attempt to create a file for writing to

```
file_ptr = fopen( "data.txt", "w" ) ;
```

Beware

Notice that both file name and file mode arguments must be enclosed within double quotes.

4. Now, output a message to confirm the attempt succeeded, then close the file and return a zero integer value as required by the function declaration

```
if( file_ptr != NULL )
{
  printf( "File created\n" ) ;
  fclose( file_ ptr ) ;
  return 0 ;
}
```

5. Finally, output an alternative message if the attempt fails

```
else
{
  printf( "Unable to create file\n" ) ; return 1 ;
}
```

Hot tip

Notice that this program returns a value of 1 to the system when the attempt to open the file fails – this tells the system that all did not go well.

6. Save the program file, then compile and execute the program to attempt to create a text file

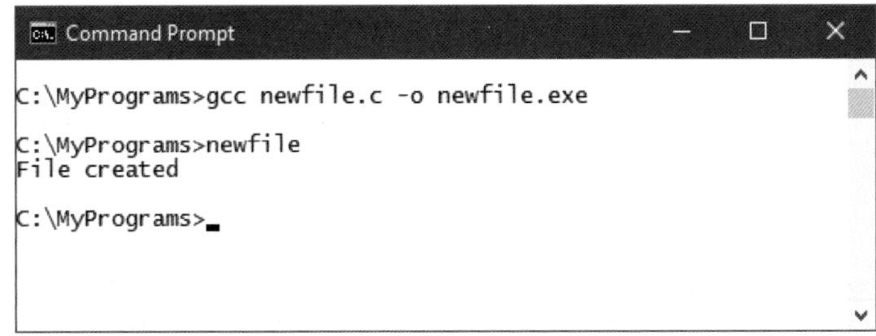
Command Prompt
C:\MyPrograms>gcc newfile.c -o newfile.exe
C:\MyPrograms>newfile
File created
C:\MyPrograms>

Reading & writing characters

Standard input

The **scanf()** function, used in previous examples, is the simplified version of a function named **fscanf()** that requires an input filestream as its first argument. This indicates a source from where a series of characters will be introduced into the program.

In C programming, the filestream named **stdin** represents the keyboard and is the default source for the **scanf()** function. The function call **scanf(...)** is the same as **fscanf(stdin, ...)** .

Standard output

Similarly, the **printf()** function is the simplified version of a function named **fprintf()** that requires an output filestream as its first argument. This indicates a destination where a series of characters will be output from the program.

The filestream named **stdout** represents the monitor, and is the default source for the **printf()** function. The function call **printf(...)** is the same as **fprintf(stdout, ...)** .

Other standard functions, which have **stdin** or **stdout** as their default filestreams, also have equivalents allowing an alternative filestream to be specified. These can be used to read files by specifying a file pointer as an alternative to reading from the **stdin** filestream. They can also be used to write files by specifying an alternative to the **stdout** filestream:

- The **fputc()** function can be used to write to a filestream one character at a time – typically by looping through a **char** array. Its companion **fgetc()** can be used to read from a filestream one character at a time.
- The **fputs()** function can be used to write to a filestream one line at a time, and its companion **fgets()** can be used to read from a filestream one line at a time.
- The **fread()** function can be used to read an entire filestream, and its partner **fwrite()** can write an entire filestream.
- The **fscanf()** function and the **fprintf()** functions can be used to read and write filestreams with strings and numbers.

Another standard output filestream named **stderr** is used to output error messages.

writechars.c

1. Begin a new program with a preprocessor instruction to include the standard input/output library functions

```
#include <stdio.h>
```

2. Add a main function that declares a file pointer, a loop counter variable, and an initialized character array

```
int main()
{
  FILE *file_ptr ; int i ;
  char text[50] = { "Text, one character at a time." } ;
}
```

3. Next, in the main function block, attempt to create a file for writing to

```
file_ptr = fopen( "chars.txt" , "w" ) ;
```

4. Now, output a message to confirm the attempt succeeded, write each character from the array, then close the file and return the required zero integer value

```
if( file_ptr != NULL )
{
  printf( "File chars.txt created\n" ) ;
  for( i = 0 ; text[i] ; i++ ) { fputc( text[i], file_ptr ) ; }
  fclose( file_ ptr ) ;
  return 0 ;
}
```

5. Finally, output an alternative message if the attempt fails

```
else { printf( "Unable to create file\n" ) ; return 1 ; }
```

6. Save the program file, then compile and execute the program to attempt to write a text file

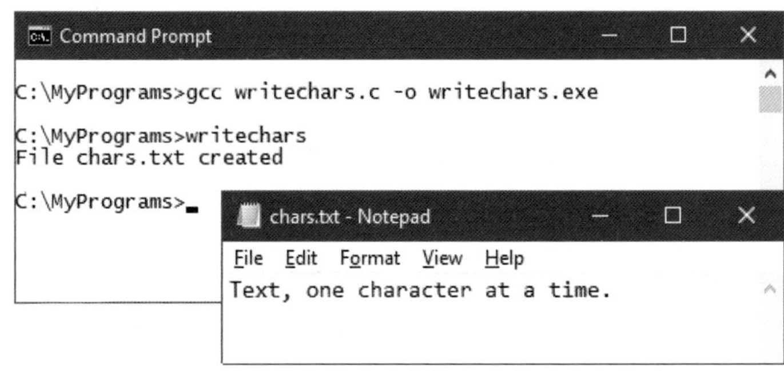

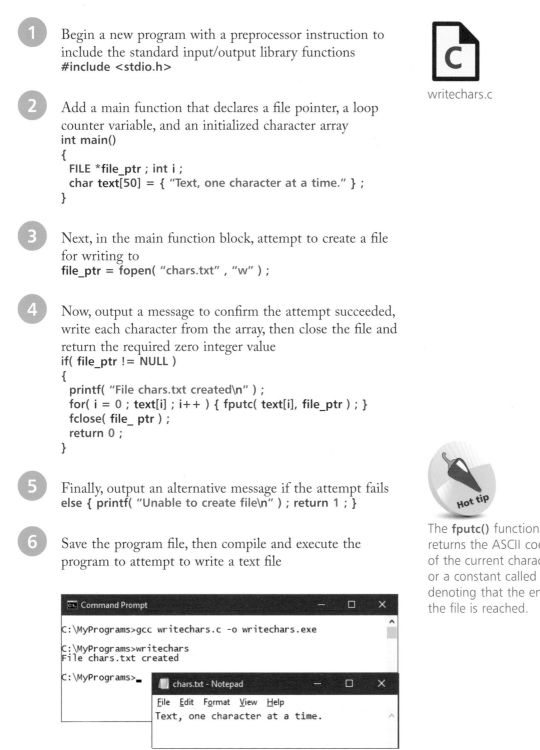

The **fputc()** function returns the ASCII code of the current character, or a constant called **EOF** denoting that the end of the file is reached.

Reading & writing lines

The **fgetc()** function is not the most efficient way to read text into a program, as it must be called repeatedly to read each character. It is better to employ the **fgets()** function that reads text one whole line at a time.

The **fgets()** function requires three arguments. The first argument specifies a **char** pointer or **char** array to which the text will be assigned. The second argument must be an integer specifying the maximum number of characters to read per line. The third argument is a file pointer specifying where to read from.

Similarly, the **fputc()** function, which writes text one character at a time, is less efficient than the **fputs()** function that writes text line by line. The **fputs()** function requires two arguments to specify the text to write and a file pointer denoting the file to be written to. A newline character is added by **fputs()** after the line is written. This function returns zero when successful, or the **EOF** constant when an error occurs or the end of the file is reached.

lines.c

1. Begin a new program with a preprocessor instruction to include the standard input/output and string functions

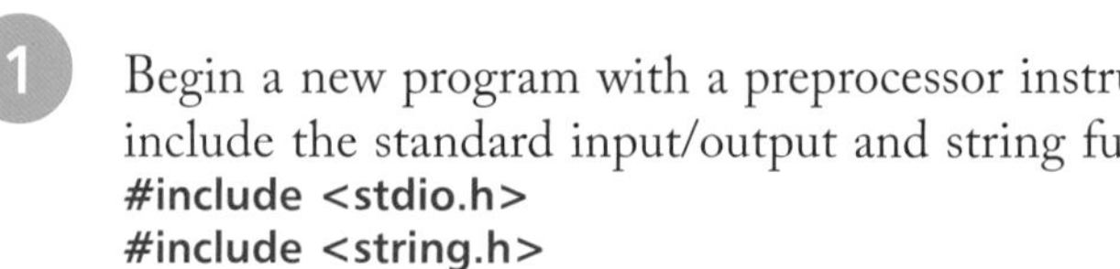

```
#include <stdio.h>
#include <string.h>
```

2. Add a main function that declares a file pointer and an uninitialized character array

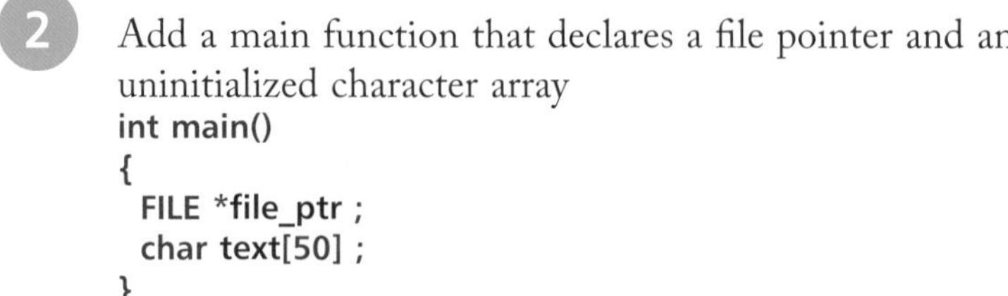

```
int main()
{
  FILE *file_ptr ;
  char text[50] ;
}
```

3. Next, in the main function block, attempt to open a local text file for both reading and appending to

```
file_ptr = fopen( "farewell.txt", "r+a" ) ;
```

farewell.txt - Notepad

File Edit Format View Help

```
A thousand suns will stream on thee,
A thousand moons will quiver;
But not by thee my steps shall be,
For ever and for ever...
```

4. Now, output a message to confirm the attempt succeeded

```
if( file_ptr != NULL )
{
  printf( "File farewell.txt opened\n" ) ;
}
```

5. Next, in the if block, read and output all lines from the file

```
while( fgets( text, 50, file_ptr ) ) { printf( "%s", text ) ; }
```

6. Now, in the if block, copy a new string to the array then append that string to the text file

```
strcpy( text , "...by Lord Alfred Tennyson" ) ;
fputs( text , file_ptr ) ;
```

7. Finally, in the if block, close the file and return the required zero integer value

```
fclose( file_ptr ) ;
return 0 ;
```

8. Add an alternative message if the attempt fails

```
else { printf( "Unable to open file\n" ) ; return 1 ; }
```

9. Save the program file, then compile and execute the program to open the file and append the text string

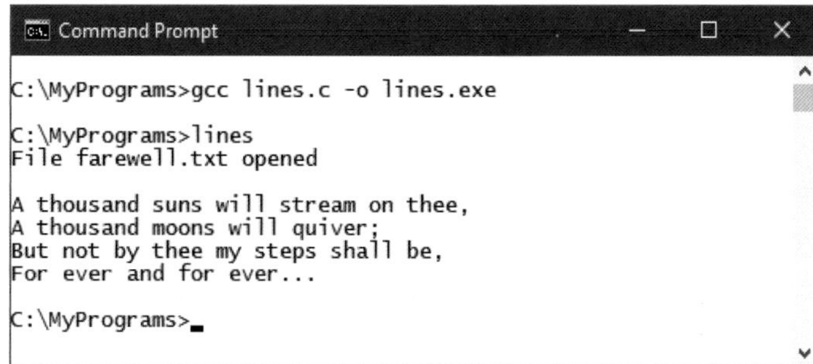
Command Prompt
C:\MyPrograms>gcc lines.c -o lines.exe
C:\MyPrograms>lines
File farewell.txt opened
A thousand suns will stream on thee,
A thousand moons will quiver;
But not by thee my steps shall be,
For ever and for ever...
C:\MyPrograms>

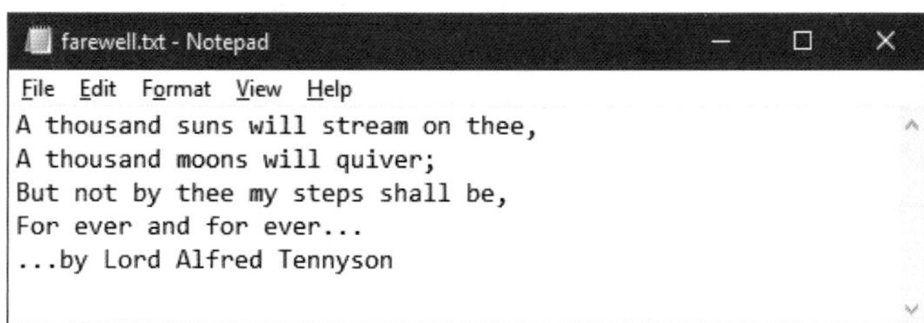
farewell.txt - Notepad
File Edit Format View Help
A thousand suns will stream on thee,
A thousand moons will quiver;
But not by thee my steps shall be,
For ever and for ever...
...by Lord Alfred Tennyson

Hot tip

Notice how the **strcpy()** function is used here to assign a new string to the **char** array.

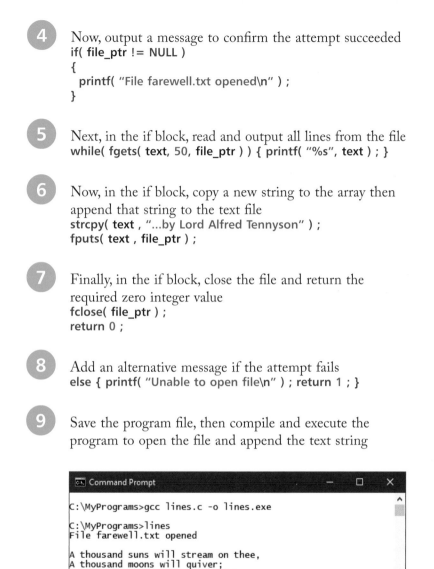

Reading & writing entire files

Whole files can be read with the **fread()** function and written with the **fwrite()** function. Both these functions take the same four arguments. The first is a **char** variable where the text can be stored. The second argument specifies the size of the chunks of text to read or write at a time – normally this will be 1. The third argument specifies the total number of characters to read or write, and the fourth argument is a file pointer to the file to work with.

The **fread()** function returns the number of objects it has read, counting characters, spaces, and newlines as one object each. Similarly, **fwrite()** returns the number of objects it has written.

readwrite.c

1. Begin a new program with a preprocessor instruction to include the standard input/output library functions

```
#include <stdio.h>
```

2. Add a main function that declares two file pointers, a character array variable, and an integer variable

```
int main()
{
  FILE *orig_ptr ;
  FILE *copy_ptr ;
  char buffer[1000] ;
  int num ;
}
```

Don't forget

The **char** array storing the text must be large enough to accommodate the entire content.

3. Next, in the main function block, attempt to open an existing local file to read and another file to write to

```
orig_ptr = fopen ( "original.txt" , "r" ) ;
copy_ptr = fopen( "copy.txt" , "w" ) ;
```

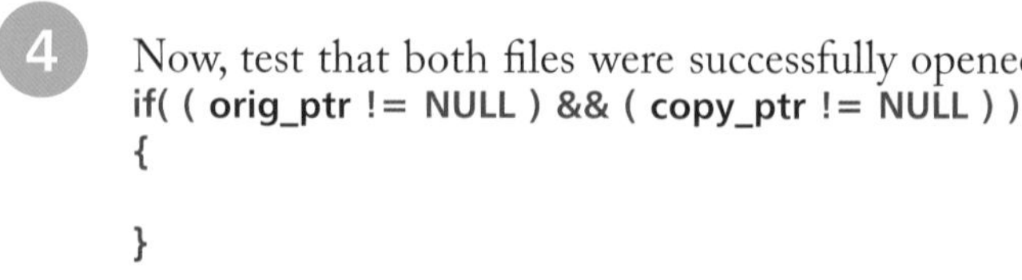
original.txt - Notepad
File Edit Format View Help
The workers have nothing to lose in this [revolution] but their chains.
They have a world to gain.
Workers of the world unite!

- Karl Marx, The Communist Manifesto 1848

4. Now, test that both files were successfully opened

```
if( ( orig_ptr != NULL ) && ( copy_ptr != NULL ) )
{

}
```

5 In the if block, read the contents from the original file into the character array, counting each object read, then write the contents of the array into the second file

```
num = fread( buffer , 1 , 1000, orig_ptr ) ;
fwrite( buffer , 1 , num , copy_ptr ) ;
```

6 Remember to close both text files upon completion

```
fclose( orig_ptr ) ;
fclose( copy_ptr ) ;
```

7 Finally, in the if block, output a confirmation, including the object count, and return the required zero integer value

```
printf( "Done: original.txt copied to copy.txt" ) ;
printf( "\n%d objects copied.\n" , num ) ;
return 0 ;
```

8 Add an alternative message for if the attempt should fail

```
else
{
  if(orig_ptr == NULL) printf( "Unable to open original.txt\n") ;
  if(copy_ptr == NULL) printf( "Unable to open copy.txt\n" ) ;
  return 1 ;
}
```

9 Save the program file, then compile and execute the program to open a file and copy its contents to a new file

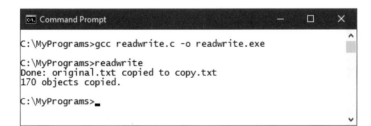

```
Command Prompt
C:\MyPrograms>gcc readwrite.c -o readwrite.exe

C:\MyPrograms>readwrite
Done: original.txt copied to copy.txt
170 objects copied.

C:\MyPrograms>
```

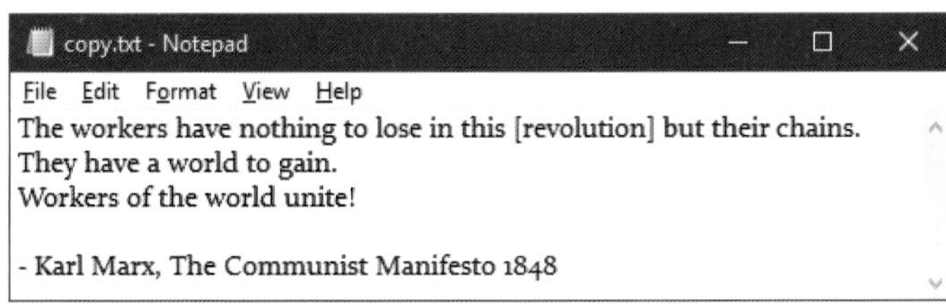
copy.txt - Notepad
File Edit Format View Help
The workers have nothing to lose in this [revolution] but their chains.
They have a world to gain.
Workers of the world unite!
- Karl Marx, The Communist Manifesto 1848

Hot tip

Use the number returned by **fread()** as the third argument to **fwrite()** to ensure that the number of objects written will be the same as the number of objects read.

Beware

Ensure that the third argument to **fread()** is big enough to allow all the contents to be copied – changing the value in this example to 100 would then only copy the first 100 objects, omitting the final 70 objects.

Scanning filestreams

The **scanf()** function, used to get user input, is a simplified version of the **fscanf()** function with its filestream constantly set to **stdin**. The **fscanf()** function allows you to nominate the filestream to read as its first argument. It also has an advantage when reading files containing just numbers – numbers in a text file are simply seen as a string of characters, but when read by **fscanf()** they can be converted to their numeric type.

Similarly, the **printf()** function, used for output, is a simplified version of the **fprintf()** function with its filestream constantly set to **stdout**. The **fprintf()** function allows you to nominate the filestream to write to as its first argument.

So **fscanf()** and **fprintf()** offer great flexibility in choosing whether to read from **stdin** or a file, and whether to write to **stdout** or a file.

fscanprint.c

1. Begin a new program with a preprocessor instruction to include the standard input/output library functions

```
#include <stdio.h>
```

2. Add a main function that declares two file pointers, an integer array variable, and two regular integer variables

```
int main()
{
  FILE *nums_ptr , *hint_ptr ;
  int nums[20] , i , j ;
}
```

3. Next, in the main function block, attempt to open an existing local file to read and another file to write to

```
nums_ptr = fopen ( "nums.txt" , "r" ) ;
hint_ptr = fopen( "hint.txt" , "w" ) ;
```

nums.txt - Notepad
File Edit Format View Help
1 2 3 4 5 6 7 8 9 10

4. Now, test that both files were successfully opened

```
if( ( nums_ptr != NULL ) && ( hint_ptr != NULL ) )
{

}
```

5 In the if block, scan the integers from the file into the elements of the integer array

```
for( i = 0 ; !feof( nums_ptr ) ; i++ )
{
   fscanf( nums_ptr , "%d" , &nums[i] ) ;
}
```

Notice that the **feof()** function is used in this example to test if the end of the file has been reached – exiting the loop when it is reached.

6 Next, in the if block, output the array element values

```
fprintf( stdout , "\nTotal numbers found: %d\n" , i ) ;
for( j=0 ; j<i ; j++ ) { fprintf( stdout , "%d " , nums[j] ) ; }
```

7 Now, write the array element values into a file

```
fprintf( hint_ptr , "fscanf and fprintf are flexible\n" ) ;
for( j=0 ; j<i ; j++ ) { fprintf( hint_ptr , "%d " , nums[j] ) ; }
```

8 Finally, in the if block, close both files upon completion

```
fclose( nums_ptr ) ;
fclose( hint_ptr ) ;
```

9 Add an alternative message for if the attempt should fail

```
else
{
  fprintf( stdout , "Unable to open a file\n" ) ; return 1 ;
}
```

10 Save the program file, then compile and execute the program to open a file then output and write its contents

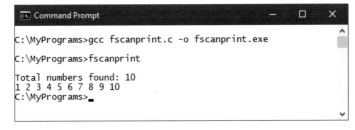

The **fscanf()** and **fprintf()** functions take the same arguments as **scanf()** and **printf()** plus an additional first stream argument.

Command Prompt

```
C:\MyPrograms>gcc fscanprint.c -o fscanprint.exe

C:\MyPrograms>fscanprint

Total numbers found: 10
1 2 3 4 5 6 7 8 9 10
C:\MyPrograms>_
```

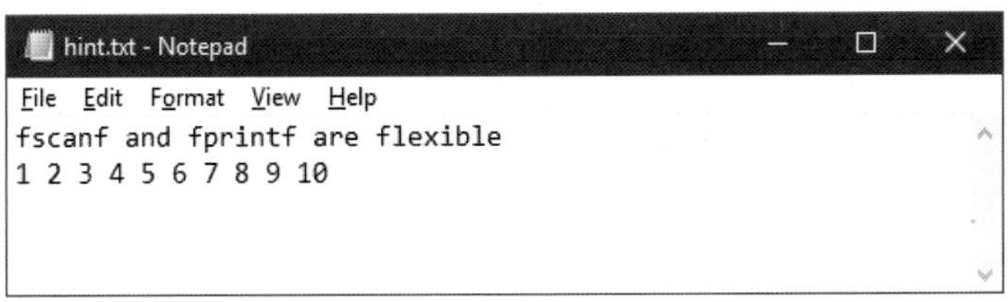
hint.txt - Notepad

File Edit Format View Help

```
fscanf and fprintf are flexible
1 2 3 4 5 6 7 8 9 10
```

Reporting errors

The C language provides a function named **perror()** in the **stdio.h** header file that can be used to print descriptive error messages. It requires a string as its sole argument, to which **perror()** adds a colon followed by a description of the current error.

Additionally, the **errno.h** header file defines an integer expression named "errno" that is assigned an error code number when an error occurs. This error code number can be specified as the argument to a **strerror()** function from the **string.h** header file to output its associated error message.

errno.c

1. Begin a new program with a preprocessor instruction to include the standard input/output functions, error message handling, and string functions

```
#include <stdio.h>
#include <errno.h>
#include <string.h>
```

2. Add a main function that declares a file pointer and an integer variable

```
int main()
{
  FILE *f_ptr ;
  int i ;
}
```

3. Next, in the main function block, attempt to open a file that does not actually exist

```
f_ptr = fopen( "nosuch.file" , "r" ) ;
```

4. Output a confirmation or an error message as the attempt has failed

```
if( f_ptr != NULL ) { printf( "File opened\n" ) ; }
else { perror( "Error" ) ; }
```

5. Now, add a loop to output the error message associated with each defined numerical errno error code

```
for( i = 0 ; i < 44 ; i++)
{
  printf( "Error %d : %s\n" , i , strerror(i) ) ;
}
```

6. At the end of the main function block, return a zero integer value, as required by the function declaration
return 0 ;

7. Save the program file, then compile and execute the program to see the error messages

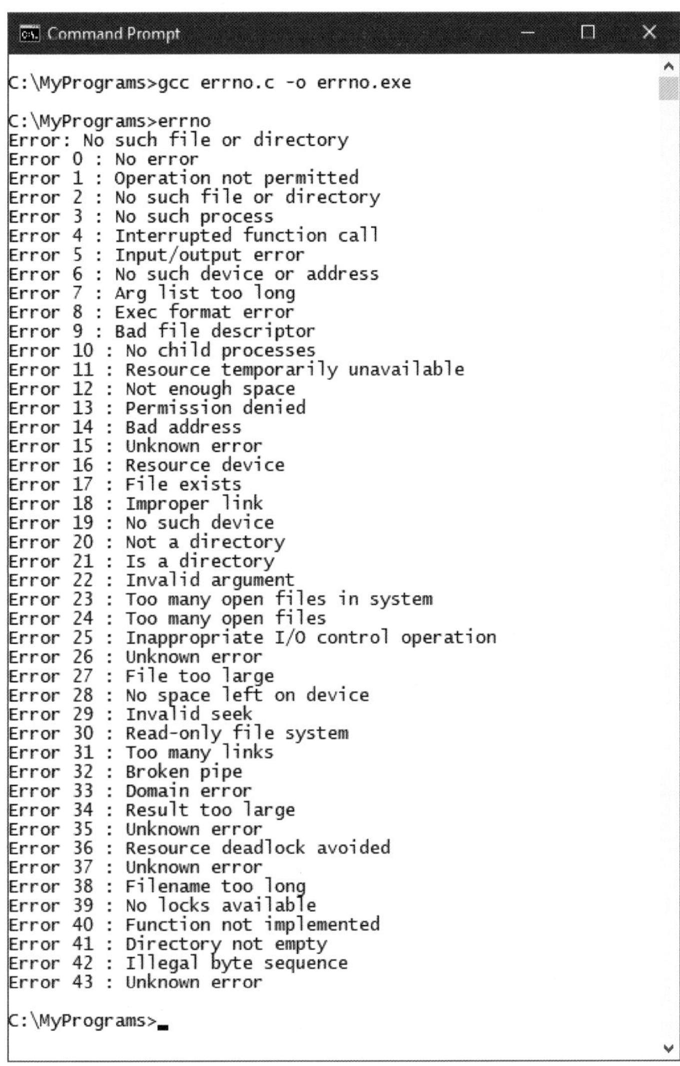
Command Prompt
C:\MyPrograms>gcc errno.c -o errno.exe
C:\MyPrograms>errno
Error: No such file or directory
Error 0 : No error
Error 1 : Operation not permitted
Error 2 : No such file or directory
Error 3 : No such process
Error 4 : Interrupted function call
Error 5 : Input/output error
Error 6 : No such device or address
Error 7 : Arg list too long
Error 8 : Exec format error
Error 9 : Bad file descriptor
Error 10 : No child processes
Error 11 : Resource temporarily unavailable
Error 12 : Not enough space
Error 13 : Permission denied
Error 14 : Bad address
Error 15 : Unknown error
Error 16 : Resource device
Error 17 : File exists
Error 18 : Improper link
Error 19 : No such device
Error 20 : Not a directory
Error 21 : Is a directory
Error 22 : Invalid argument
Error 23 : Too many open files in system
Error 24 : Too many open files
Error 25 : Inappropriate I/O control operation
Error 26 : Unknown error
Error 27 : File too large
Error 28 : No space left on device
Error 29 : Invalid seek
Error 30 : Read-only file system
Error 31 : Too many links
Error 32 : Broken pipe
Error 33 : Domain error
Error 34 : Result too large
Error 35 : Unknown error
Error 36 : Resource deadlock avoided
Error 37 : Unknown error
Error 38 : Filename too long
Error 39 : No locks available
Error 40 : Function not implemented
Error 41 : Directory not empty
Error 42 : Illegal byte sequence
Error 43 : Unknown error
C:\MyPrograms>

Hot tip

The range of error code messages is implementation-defined. The range is larger on Linux systems than for the Windows platform.

Getting the date and time

Current system time is usually counted as the number of seconds elapsed since the Epoch at 00:00:00 GMT on January 1, 1970. The total count represents the current date and time according to the Gregorian calendar and is referred to as "Calendar time". Special functions to handle date and time are provided in the **time.h** header file along with a data type struct named **tm** in which to store date and time components, as below:

Component:	Description:
int tm_sec	seconds after the minute, normally 0-59
int tm_min	minutes after the hour, 0-59
int tm_hour	hours since midnight, 0-23
int tm_mday	day of the month, 1-31
int tm_mon	months since January, 0-11
int tm_year	years since 1900
int tm_wday	days since Sunday, 0-6
int tm_yday	days since January 1st, 0-365
int tm_isdst	is Daylight Saving Time in effect

The Daylight Saving component **tm_isdst** is positive if Daylight Saving is in effect; zero if not; or negative if that information is unavailable.

The current elapsed seconds count is returned by a **time(NULL)** function as a **time_t** data type. This can then be specified as the argument to a **localtime()** function for conversion to its various **tm** struct components.

A complete list of all time format specifiers is included in the Reference section on page 183.

The struct components can be output in a standard date and time format using an **asctime()** function. Alternatively, individual components can be output using special time format specifiers with a **strftime()** function. This function requires four arguments to specify a **char** array in which to store the formatted date string, the maximum string length, the text and format specifiers to extract the required components, and the **tm** struct to be used.

datetime.c

1. Begin a new program with a preprocessor instruction to include the standard input/output library functions and the date and time functions

```
#include <stdio.h>
#include <time.h>
```

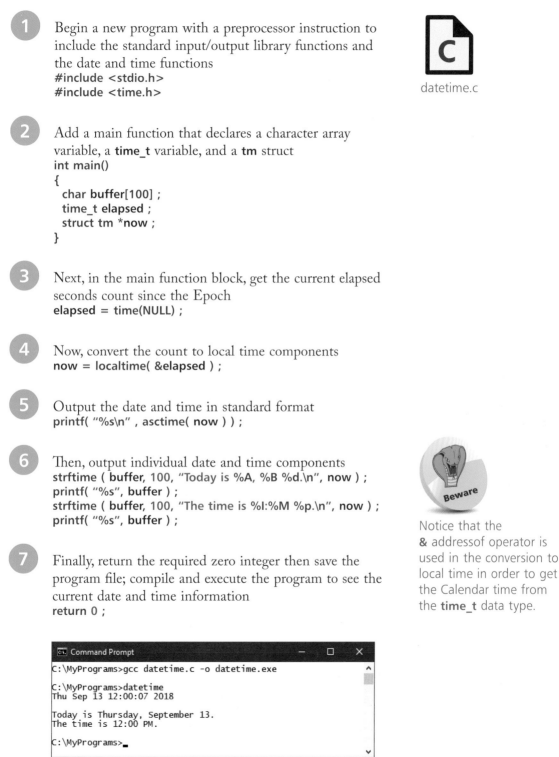

2. Add a main function that declares a character array variable, a **time_t** variable, and a **tm** struct

```
int main()
{
  char buffer[100] ;
  time_t elapsed ;
  struct tm *now ;
}
```

3. Next, in the main function block, get the current elapsed seconds count since the Epoch

```
elapsed = time(NULL) ;
```

4. Now, convert the count to local time components

```
now = localtime( &elapsed ) ;
```

5. Output the date and time in standard format

```
printf( "%s\n" , asctime( now ) ) ;
```

6. Then, output individual date and time components

```
strftime ( buffer, 100, "Today is %A, %B %d.\n", now ) ;
printf( "%s", buffer ) ;
strftime ( buffer, 100, "The time is %I:%M %p.\n", now ) ;
printf( "%s", buffer ) ;
```

7. Finally, return the required zero integer then save the program file; compile and execute the program to see the current date and time information

```
return 0 ;
```

Notice that the **&** addressof operator is used in the conversion to local time in order to get the Calendar time from the **time_t** data type.

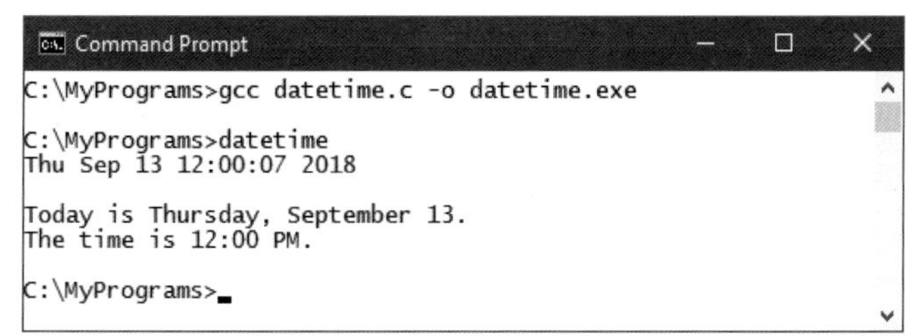

Command Prompt
C:\MyPrograms>gcc datetime.c -o datetime.exe
C:\MyPrograms>datetime
Thu Sep 13 12:00:07 2018
Today is Thursday, September 13.
The time is 12:00 PM.
C:\MyPrograms>

Running a timer

Getting the current time both before and after an event means that the duration of the event can be calculated by their difference. The **time.h** header file contains a **difftime()** function for that particular purpose. This function requires two arguments, both of which are of the **time_t** data type. It subtracts the second argument from the first argument and returns the difference expressed in whole seconds, but as a **double** data type.

Another way to work with time is offered by the **clock()** function from the **time.h** header file. This returns the processor time used since the program began, expressed in clock "ticks". This function can be used to "pause" the execution of a program by running an empty loop until a future point in time is reached.

wait.c

1. Begin a new program with a preprocessor instruction to include the standard input/output library functions and the date and time functions

```
#include <stdio.h>
#include <time.h>
```

2. Next, declare a function prototype to pause the program

```
void wait( int seconds ) ;
```

3. Add a main function that declares two **time_t** variables, and an integer variable

```
int main()
{
  time_t go , stop ;
  int i ;
}
```

4. Next, in the main function block, get the current time and output a message

```
go = time( NULL ) ;
printf ( "\nStarting countdown...\n\n" ) ;
```

5. Add a loop to output a countdown value and call the other function on each iteration

```
for( i = 10 ; i > -1 ; i-- )
{
  printf ( " - %d", i ) ;
  wait(1) ;
}
```

6. Next, in the main function block, get the current time once more then output the time taken to run the loop
```
stop = time( NULL ) ;
printf("\nRuntime: %.0f seconds\n" , difftime( stop, go ) ) ;
```

7. Finally, in the main function block, return a zero integer value, as required by the function declaration
```
return 0 ;
```

8. After the main function block, begin the function definition by initializing a **clock_t** variable at a future point beyond the current elapsed running time
```
void wait( int seconds )
{
  clock_t end_wait =
                      ( clock() + ( seconds * CLOCKS_PER_SEC ) );
}
```

9. Finally, in the wait function block, add an empty loop that terminates when the current time reaches the future point, returning control to the loop in the main function
```
while ( clock() < end_wait ) { }
```

10. Save the program file, then compile and execute the program to see the countdown timer and runtime

```
Command Prompt - wait
C:\MyPrograms>gcc wait.c -o wait.exe
C:\MyPrograms>wait
Starting countdown...
 - 10 - 9 - 8
```

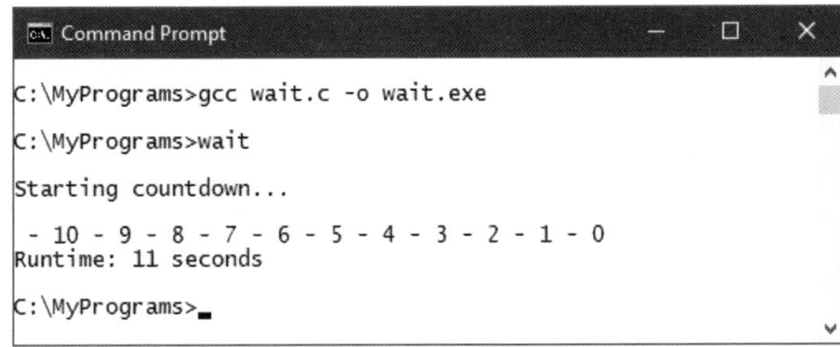

The number of clock ticks per second is implementation-dependent but is defined in **time.h** by the **CLOCKS_PER_SEC** constant.

You can find the elapsed runtime expressed in seconds by dividing the value returned by the **clock()** function by the **CLOCKS_PER_SEC** value.

Generating random numbers

The **stdlib.h** header file provides a **rand()** function that generates a pseudo-random positive integer when called. This will, by default, return a number in the range from 0 to a large value (at least 32,767). A specific range can be set by using the modulus operator to specify a maximum upper limit – for example, to specify a range from 0 to 9 with the expression **rand() % 9**.

To set a minimum lower limit for the range, its value can be added to the result of the expression – for example, to specify a range from 1 to 10 with the expression **(rand() % 9) + 1**.

The numbers generated by the **rand()** function are not truly random, as the function successively generates the same sequence of numbers each time a program using **rand()** is executed. In order to generate a different sequence of numbers, the "seed" that starts the sequence must be specified. By default, the initial seed value is 1, but this can be changed by specifying an alternative integer argument to the **srand()** function – for example, **srand(8)**. This will cause **rand()** to generate a different sequence of numbers to those generated using the default seed value, but the sequence will still be repeated each time a program using **rand()** is executed.

To generate different random sequences upon successive execution the argument specified to **srand()** must be something other than a static integer. The common solution is to seed the **rand()** function with the current time in elapsed seconds with **srand(time(NULL))**.

Now, the sequence of numbers generated by **rand()** will be different each time a program using **rand()** is executed.

lotto.c

1. Begin a new program with preprocessor instructions to include the standard input/output library functions, random number, time, and string functions

```
#include <stdio.h>
#include <stdlib.h>
#include <time.h>
#include <string.h>
```

2. Add a main function that declares **int** and **char** variables

```
int main()
{
  int i , r , temp , nums[60] ;
  char buf[4], str[100]= { "Your Six Lucky Numbers Are: " } ;
}
```

3 In the main function block, first seed the random number generator with the current elapsed seconds value

```
srand( time(NULL) ) ;
```

4 Next, fill an array with the numbers 0-59 in sequence

```
for( i = 0 ; i < 60 ; i++ ) { nums[i] = i ; }
```

5 Now, shuffle the sequence into a random order

```
for( i = 1 ; i < 60 ; i++ )
{
  r = ( rand() % 59 ) + 1 ;
  temp = nums[i] ; nums[i]=nums[r] ; nums[r] = temp ;
}
```

6 Add the numbers from six array elements to a string

```
for( i = 1 ; i < 7 ; i++ )
{
  sprintf( buf, "%d ", nums[i] ) ;
  strcat( buf , " " ) ; strcat( str , buf ) ;
}
```

7 Then, output the string

```
printf( "\n%s\n\n" , str ) ;
```

8 At the end of the main function block, return a zero integer value, as required by the function declaration

```
return 0 ;
```

9 Save the program file, then compile and execute the program repeatedly to see a selection of six different random numbers in the range 1-59 upon each execution

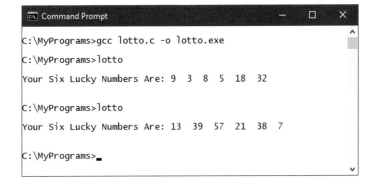

```
Command Prompt
C:\MyPrograms>gcc lotto.c -o lotto.exe
C:\MyPrograms>lotto
Your Six Lucky Numbers Are: 9  3  8  5  18  32

C:\MyPrograms>lotto
Your Six Lucky Numbers Are: 13  39  57  21  38  7

C:\MyPrograms>_
```

The array element **nums[0]** gets assigned a zero value, but this is not included in the shuffle as only elements 1-59 are eligible for selection.

Notice how the **sprintf()** function is used here to translate **int** values into **char** values that can then be concatenated to the larger text string.

Displaying a dialog box

In the Windows operating system, C programs can easily produce graphical components via special functions provided by the Windows Application Programming Interface (WINAPI). This is made available to the program by adding a compiler directive to include the Windows-specific **windows.h** header file.

Notice that the **WinMain()** function requires an integer to be returned upon completion, just like the usual **main()** function.

In a C program for Windows, the usual **main()** function program entry point is replaced by this special **WinMain()** function:

int WINAPI WinMain(HINSTANCE *hInstance*,
HINSTANCE *hPrevInstance*, LPSTR *lpCmdLine*, int *nCmdShow*)

These arguments are always required in order for the program to communicate with the operating system. The ***hInstance*** argument is a "handle" reference to the program; and the ***hPrevInstance*** argument, used in earlier Windows programming, can be safely ignored these days. The ***lpCmdLine*** argument is a string that represents all items used on the command line to compile the application, and the ***nCmdShow*** argument controls how the window will be displayed.

The most simple graphical component to create in Windows is a basic dialog box with just one "OK" button. This is created by calling this **MessageBox()** function:

int MessageBox(HWND *hWnd*, LPCTSTR *lpText*,
LPCTSTR *lpCaption*, UINT *uType*);

Other MessageBox icon constants include **MB_ICONERROR**, **MB_ICONQUESTION** and **MB_ICONINFORMATION**.

The ***hWnd*** argument is a "handle" reference to the parent window, if any – without a parent window this value is specified as **NULL**. The ***lpText*** argument is the message string to be displayed, and the ***lpCaption*** argument is the title to be displayed on the dialog box. Finally, the ***uType*** argument can specify icons and buttons using special constant values in a pipe-delimited list. For example, the constant **MB_OK** adds an OK button and an exclamation icon can be added with the constant **MB_ICONEXCLAMATION**.

After compilation, a C program that creates a dialog box can be run as usual from the command line. Additionally, it can be run by a double-click on its executable file icon – but this will open both a Command Prompt window and the dialog box. But the GNU C Compiler has a special **-mwindows** option that can be added at the very end of the compilation command to suppress the Command Prompt window when the program is run by a double-click.

1. Make a copy of the previous example, **lotto.c**, and rename it as **winlotto.c**

2. At the start of the renamed program file, insert a further preprocessor instruction to make the WINAPI available
#include <windows.h>

3. Next, replace the line containing **int main()** with the one that communicates with the Windows operating system
```
int WINAPI WinMain( HINSTANCE hInstance, HINSTANCE
            hPrevInstance, LPSTR lpCmdLine, int nCmdShow)
```

4. Now, replace the call to **printf()** that outputs the selected numbers with a call that displays them in a dialog box
```
MessageBox(NULL, str, "Lotto Number Picker",
                    MB_OK | MB_ICONEXCLAMATION );
```

5. Save the program file, compile the program using the special compiler option, then run the program – both from the command line and by a double-click

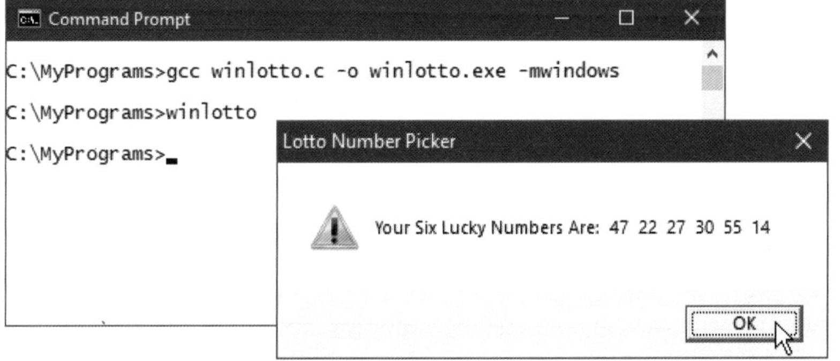

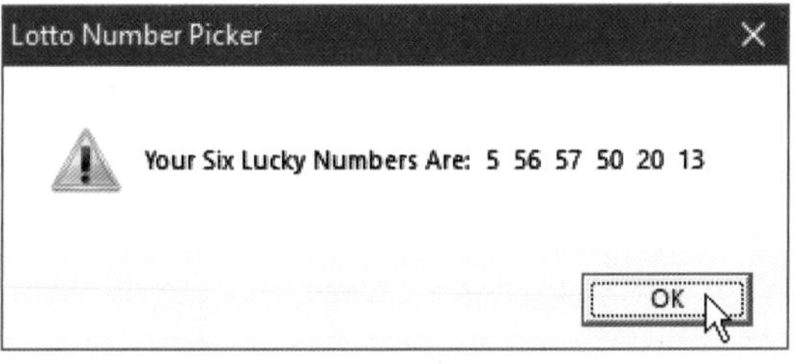

Summary

- A file pointer has the syntax **FILE** ***fp*** and can be used to open, read, write, and close files.
- The **fopen()** function that opens files must state the file location and a file mode as its two arguments.
- After completing operations on a file, that file must then be closed by the **fclose()** function.
- Individual characters are read and written with **fgetc()** and **fputc()**, but **fgets()** and **fputs()** read and write whole lines.
- The **fread()** and **fwrite()** functions can read and write entire filestreams into and out from character buffers.
- Flexibility is offered by the **fscanf()** and **fprintf()** functions that can read and write to a filestream, **stdin**, or **stdout**.
- Error messages can be written by the **perror()** function, or the **strerror()** function can write a message associated with **errno**.
- The number of seconds elapsed since the Epoch at midnight on January 1, 1970 is returned by calling **time(NULL)**.
- Members of a **tm struct** are initialized by converting the elapsed seconds count with the **localtime()** function.
- A standard date and time format is provided by the **asctime()** function, but individual components can be formatted using format specifiers with the **strftime()** function.
- Time points during the execution of a program can be established using the **difftime()** or **clock()** functions.
- The sequence of pseudo-random numbers generated by **rand()** is best first seeded with the **srand()** function and **time(NULL)**.
- Including the **windows.h** header file in a program makes the Windows API available to create graphical components.
- The entry point of a Windows program is the **WinMain()** function, and **MessageBox()** creates a simple dialog box.

Reference Section

This section of the book lists the standard ASCII key codes and every function contained in the standard C library, grouped by their header file, and also descriptions of all the standard constants.

162 ASCII character codes

164 Input & output functions <stdio.h>

173 Character test functions <ctype.h>

174 String functions <string.h>

176 Math functions <math.h>

178 Utility functions <stdlib.h>

180 Diagnostic functions <assert.h>

180 Argument functions <stdarg.h>

181 Date & time functions <time.h>

184 Jump functions <setjmp.h>

184 Signal functions <signal.h>

185 Limit constants <limits.h>

186 Float constants <float.h>

ASCII character codes

ASCII (American Standard Code for Information Interchange) is the standard representation of characters by numerical code. The non-printing character codes, originally developed for teletypes, are now rarely used for their intended original purpose.

There are also extended ASCII code sets from 128-255 (not listed) containing accented characters and symbols, but these sets do vary.

Note that the character represented by character code 32 is not missing – it is, in fact, the non-printing space character. Also, the character represented by character code 127 is the delete character.

Code:	Char:	Description:
0	NUL	null
1	SOH	start of heading
2	STX	start of text
3	ETX	end of text
4	EOT	end of transmission
5	ENQ	enquiry
6	ACK	acknowledgement
7	BEL	bell
8	BS	backspace
9	TAB	horizontal tab
10	NL	newline
11	VT	vertical tab
12	FF	form feed
13	CR	carriage return
14	SO	shift out
15	SI	shift in

Code:	Char:	Description:
16	DLE	data link escape
17	DC1	device control 1
18	DC2	device control 2
19	DC3	device control 3
20	DC4	device control 4
21	NAK	neg. acknowledge
22	SYN	synchronous file
23	ETB	end of trans. block
24	CAN	cancel
25	EM	end of medium
26	SUB	substitute
27	ESC	escape
28	FS	file separator
29	GS	group separator
30	RS	record separator
31	US	unit separator

Code:	Char:	Code:	Char:	Code:	Char:	Code:	Char:
32		56	8	80	P	104	h
33	!	57	9	81	Q	105	i
34	"	58	:	82	R	106	j
35	#	59	;	83	S	107	k
36	$	60	<	84	T	108	l
37	%	61	=	85	U	109	m
38	&	62	>	86	V	110	n
39	'	63	?	87	W	111	o
40	(	64	@	88	X	112	p
41	)	65	A	89	Y	113	q
42	*	66	B	90	Z	114	r
43	+	67	C	91	[	115	s
44	,	68	D	92	\	116	t
45	-	69	E	93	]	117	u
46	.	70	F	94	^	118	v
47	/	71	G	95	_	119	w
48	0	72	H	96	`	120	x
49	1	73	I	97	a	121	y
50	2	74	J	98	b	122	z
51	3	75	K	99	c	123	{
52	4	76	L	100	d	124	|
53	5	77	M	101	e	125	}
54	6	78	N	102	f	126	~
55	7	79	O	103	g	127	del

To find out more about extended ASCII sets try the website at **asciitable.com**, or search for "ASCII" online.

The term "ASCII file" just means a plain text file, such as those produced by Windows' Notepad application.

<stdio.h>

Input & output functions

The functions and types defined in the **stdio.h** header file represent almost one third of the C language library. It is used to introduce data into a program and generate output from a program.

A "stream" is a data source terminated by a **\n** newline character. It may be read or written by "opening" the stream, and terminated by "closing" it. Opening a stream returns a **FILE** type pointer in which information needed to control the stream is stored.

The functions listed in the following table perform file operations:

File-handling functions

FILE fopen(const char **filename* , const char *mode*)

The **fopen()** function returns a **FILE** pointer, or **NULL** if the file cannot be opened. Any of the following modes may be specified in the function call:

r	open a text file for reading only
w	create a text file to write to, and discard any previous contents
a	append – open or create a text file for writing at the end of the file
r+	open a text file to update (read and write)
w+	open a text file to update (read and write, discarding any previous contents)
a+	append – open or create a text file for update, for writing at the end of the file

If the file being opened is a binary file, a **b** should be added after the file mode – for example, **wb+**

FILE freopen(const char **filename* , const char *mode* , FILE **stream*)

The **freopen()** function opens a file with the specified mode and associates the stream with it. It returns the stream, or **NULL** if an error occurs. This function is normally used to change the files associated **stdin**, **stdout** or **stderr**

int fflush(FILE **stream*)

On an output stream this function causes any buffered data to be written immediately. It returns the **EOF** constant for a write error, or zero otherwise. A call to **fflush(NULL)** flushes all output streams

int fclose(FILE **stream*)

A call to **fclose()** flushes any unwritten data from the stream then closes the stream. It returns the **EOF** constant if an error occurs, or zero otherwise

int remove(const char **filename*)

This function removes the specified file – so that any subsequent attempt to open that file will fail. It returns a non-zero value if it cannot remove the file

int rename(const char **old-name* , const char **new-name*)

The **rename()** function changes the name of the specified file, or it returns a non-zero value if it cannot rename the file

FILE *tmpfile(void)

Calling **tmpfile()** creates a temporary file, with the file mode of **wb+**, that is removed when the program ends. This function returns a stream, or **NULL** if the file cannot be created

char *tmpnam(char *arr*[*L_tmpnam*])

This function stores a string in an array and returns a unique valid name pointer to that array. The ***arr*** array must have at least ***L_tmpnam*** characters. The **tmpnam()** function generates a different name each time it is called

int setvbuf(FILE **stream* , char **buffer* , int mode , size_t *size*)

A call to **setvbuf()** sets buffering for the specified stream. It should be called after a stream has been opened but before any operation has been performed on it. Valid modes are **_IOFBF** to cause full buffering, **_IOLBF** for line buffering, and **_IONBF** for no buffering. The ***size*** sets the buffer size. This function returns a non-zero value if an error occurs

void setbuf(FILE **stream* , char **buffer*)

The **setbuf()** function defines how a stream should be buffered. It should be called after a stream has been opened but before any operation has been performed on it. The argument ***buffer*** points to an array to be used as the buffer

<stdio.h> ...cont'd

Functions that format output

int fprintf(FILE *_stream_ , const char *_format_ , ...)

The **fprintf()** function converts and writes output to a specified filestream under the control of a format specifier. It returns the number of characters written, or a negative value if an error occurs

int printf(const char *_format_ , ...)

The **printf()** function writes and converts output to **stdout**. It is equivalent to **fprintf(stdout , const char *_format_)**

int sprintf(char *_s_ , const char *_format_ , ...)

The **sprintf()** function is the same as **printf()** except the output is written into the specified string, and terminated with a **\0** null character

vprintf(const char *_format_ va_list _arg_)
vfprintf(FILE *_stream_ , const char *_format_ , va_list _arg_)
vsprintf(char *_s_ , const char *_format_ , va_list _arg_)

These three functions are equivalent to the corresponding **printf()** functions except that their variable argument list is replaced by an argument of the **va_list** type. Refer to the **stdarg.h** header file functions on page 180 for more details

Functions that format input

int fscanf(FILE *_stream_ , const char *_format_ , ...)

The **fscanf()** function reads from a specified stream under the control of a format specifier and assigns converted values to subsequent arguments. It returns the number of input items converted or the **EOF** constant if the end of the file is met, or if an error occurs

int scanf(const char *_format_ , ...)

The **scanf()** function reads and converts input to **stdin**. It is equivalent to **fscanf(stdin , const char *_format_)**

int sscanf(char *s , const char *_format_ , ...)

The **sscanf()** function is the same as **scanf()** except the input is read from the specified string

Format specifiers for output

In C, a **%** prefix denotes a format specifier. All **printf()** format specifiers are listed below, and those for **scanf()** on page 168.

Character:	printf() converts to:
d , i	**int** data type, signed decimal
o	int data type, unsigned octal without a leading zero
x , X	**int** unsigned hexadecimal. **0x** uses lowercase, such as **0xff**, and **0X** uses uppercase, such as **0XFF**
u	**int** data type, unsigned decimal
c	**int** single character, after conversion to **char** data type
s	**char** pointer to string, ending with the **\0** null character
f	**double** data type in the form xxx.yyyyyy where the number of digits after the decimal point is set by precision. The default precision is 6 digits
e , E	**double** data type in the form xx.yyyyyye±zz or xx.yyyyyyE±zz where the number of digits after the decimal point is set by precision. The default precision is 6 digits
g , G	**double** data type printed as %e or %E conversion or %f conversion, whichever is shorter
p	the memory address of a pointer
n	not a conversion, but stores the number of characters written so far by the call to the **printf()** function in an int pointer argument
%	not a conversion; prints a %

<stdio.h> …cont'd

Format specifiers for input

Character:	scanf() converts to:
d	**int** data type, signed decimal integer
i	**int** data type, which may be in octal (leading **0**) or hexadecimal (leading **0x** or **0X**)
o	**int** data type, octal integer with or without a leading zero
u	**int** data type, unsigned decimal
x	**int** hexadecimal integer, with or without leading **0x** or **0X**
c	**char** characters, into a specified array. Reads the number of characters stated in its width field (default is 1) without adding a final **\0** null character. Stops reading when a space is met
s	a string of non-whitespace **char** characters into an array. The array must be big enough for all the characters plus a final **\0** null character
e , f , g	**float** data type, optionally beginning with a sign, then followed by a string of numbers. These may contain a decimal point, and an optional exponent field containing an "E" or "e" followed by a possibly signed integer
p	a memory address, in the same form as that output by the **%p** conversion with **printf()**
n	not a conversion, but stores the number of characters read so far by the call to **scanf()** function in an **int** pointer argument
[...]	matches a string specified in the square brackets to those in the input stream and adds a **\0** null character
[^...]	matches all ASCII characters in the input stream except those specified in the square brackets, and adds a **\0** null character

Functions for character input and output

int fgetc(FILE **stream*)
Returns the next character of the specified stream as a **char**, or the **EOF** constant if at the end of the file or if an error occurs

char *fgets(char **s* , int *n* , FILE **stream*)
Reads the next ***n*** -1 characters into the specified stream then adds a **\0** null character at the end of the array. This function returns ***s***, or **NULL** if at the end of the file or if an error occurs

int fputc(int *c* , FILE **stream*)
Writes the character ***c*** to the specified stream and returns the character written or **EOF** if an error occurs

int fputs(const char **s* , FILE **stream*)
Writes the string ***s*** to the specified stream and returns a non-negative value, or **EOF** if an error occurs

int getc(FILE **stream*)
The **getc()** function is the macro equivalent of **fgetc()**

int getchar(void)
The **getchar()** function is equivalent to **getc(stdin)**

char *gets(char **s*)
Reads the next input line into an array, replacing its final newline character with a **\0** null character. It returns ***s***, or **NULL** if at the end of the file or if an error occurs

int putc(int *c* , FILE **stream*)
The **putc()** function is the macro equivalent of **fputc()**

int putchar(int c) is equivalent to **putc(*c* , stdout)**

int puts(const char **s*)
Writes the string ***s*** and a newline character to **stdout**. It returns a non-negative value, or **EOF** if an error occurs

int ungetc(int *c* , FILE **stream*)
Pushes the character ***c*** back onto the specified stream where it is returned on the next read. Only one pushback character per stream is guaranteed and **EOF** cannot be pushed back. This function returns the character pushed back, or **EOF** if an error occurs

...cont'd

Functions for direct stream input and output

The **fread()** and **fwrite()** functions contained in the **stdio.h** header file are most effective to read and write entire text files:

size_t fread(void **ptr* , size_t *size* , size_t *nobj* , FILE **stream*)

The **fread()** function reads from the specified stream into the specified ***ptr*** array pointer at most ***nobj*** objects of ***size*** size. This function returns the number of objects it has read, which may be less than the number requested in the function call.

The status of **fread()** can be tested as it proceeds using the **feof()** function and **ferror()** functions – see the error functions listed on the opposite page

size_t fwrite(const void **ptr*, size_t *size*, size_t *nobj*, FILE **stream*)

The **fwrite()** function writes from the specified ***ptr*** pointer ***nobj*** objects of ***size*** size. It returns the number of objects that it has written. If an error occurs, the returned value will be less than that requested by ***nobj*** in the function call

Error functions

Many of the standard functions in the C library set status indicators when an error occurs, or when the end of a file is reached. These indicators can be tested using the error functions listed in the table below. Also, the integer expression **errno**, defined in the **errno.h** header file, may contain an error code giving more information about the most recent error.

void clearerr(FILE *_stream_)
The **clearerr()** function clears the end of file and error indicators for the specified stream
int feof(FILE *_stream_)
The **feof()** function returns a non-zero value if the end of file indicator is set for the specified stream
int ferror(FILE *_stream_)
The **ferror()** function returns a non-zero value if the error indicator is set for the specified stream
void perror(const char *_s_)
The **perror()** function prints an implementation-defined error message associated with the integer value contained in the **errno** expression. See also the **strerror()** function in the **string.h** header file

File-positioning functions

A filestream is processed by moving through the characters it contains, one by one. The functions in the following table can be used to manipulate the position in the filestream:

int fseek(FILE **stream* , long *offset* , int *original*)
The **fseek()** function sets the file position in the specified stream. Subsequent reading or writing begins at the new position. The new position is determined by specifying how far to ***offset*** the position from its ***original*** position. Optionally, the third argument of this function can be specified as **SEEK_SET** (beginning), **SEEK_CUR** (current position), or **SEEK_END** (end of file). For a text stream the offset must be either zero or a value returned by the **ftell()** function, with the original position specified as **SEEK_SET**. The **fseek()** function returns non-zero if an error occurs
long ftell(FILE **stream*)
The **ftell()** function returns the current file position of the specified stream, or -1 if an error occurs
int fgetpos(FILE **stream* , fpos_t **ptr*)
The **fgetpos()** function records the current file position of the specified stream in the specified ***ptr*** pointer as a special **fpos_t** type. This function returns a non-zero value if an error occurs
int fsetpos(FILE **stream* , const fpos_t **ptr*)
The **fsetpos()** function positions the file pointer in the specified stream at the position recorded by **fgetpos()** in the ***ptr*** pointer. This function returns a non-zero value if an error occurs

Character test functions

The **ctype.h** header file contains functions for testing characters. In each case, the character must be specified as the function's argument. The function returns a non-zero value (true) when the tested condition is met, or zero (false) if it is not. Additionally, this header file contains two functions for converting the case of letters. All the functions in the **ctype.h** header file are listed in the table below, together with a description of their purpose:

Function:	Description:
isalpha(***c*** **)**	is the character a letter?
isalnum(***c*** **)**	is the character a letter or a number?
iscntrl(***c*** **)**	is the character a control character?
isdigit(***c*** **)**	is the character a decimal digit?
isgraph(***c*** **)**	is the character any printing character except a space?
islower(***c*** **)**	is the character a lowercase letter?
isprint(***c*** **)**	is the character any printing character including a space?
ispunct(***c*** **)**	is the character any printing character except a space, a letter, or a digit?
isspace(***c*** **)**	is the character a space, formfeed, newline, carriage return, horizontal tab, or vertical tab?
isupper(***c*** **)**	is the character an uppercase letter?
isxdigit(***c*** **)**	is the character a hexadecimal digit?
int tolower(int ***c*** **)**	convert the character to lowercase
int toupper(int ***c*** **)**	convert the character to uppercase

String functions

The **string.h** header file contains the following functions that can be used to compare and manipulate text strings:

Function:	Description:
char *strcpy(*s1* , *s2*)	copy ***s2*** to ***s1***, then return ***s1***
char *strncpy(*s1* , *s2* , *n*)	copy ***n*** characters of ***s2*** to ***s1***, then return ***s1***
char *strcat(*s1* , *s2*)	concatenate ***s2*** to the end of ***s1***, then return ***s1***
char *strncat(*s1* , *s2* , *n*)	concatenate ***n*** characters of ***s2*** to the end of ***s1***, then return ***s1***
int strcmp(*s1* , *s2*)	compare ***s1*** to ***s2***, then return **< 0** if ***s1 < s2***, or **0** if ***s1 == s2***, or **> 0** if ***s1 > s2***
int strncmp(*s1* , *s2* , *n*)	compare ***n*** characters of ***s1*** to ***s2***, then return **< 0** if ***s1 < s2***, or **0** if ***s1 == s2***, or **> 0** if ***s1 > s2***
char *strchr(*s* , *c*)	return a pointer to the first occurrence of ***c*** in ***s***, or **NULL** if not present
char *strrchr(*s* , *c*)	return a pointer to the last occurrence of ***c*** in ***s***, or **NULL** if not present
size_t strspn(*s1* , *s2*)	return length of prefix of ***s1*** consisting of characters in ***s2***
size_t strcspn(*s1* , *s2*)	return length of prefix of ***s1*** consisting of characters not in ***s2***

Function:	Description:
char *strpbrk(*s1* , *s2*)	return a pointer to the first occurrence in ***s1*** of any character of ***s2***, or **NULL** if none are present
char *strstr(*s1* , *s2*)	return a pointer to the first occurrence of ***s2*** in ***s1***, or **NULL** if not present
size_t strlen(*s*)	return the length of ***s***
char *strerror(*n*)	return a pointer to the implementation-defined string associated with error code ***n***
char *strtok(*s1* , *s2*)	search ***s1*** for tokens delimited by characters from ***s2***
void *memcpy(*s1* , *s2* , *n*)	copy ***n*** characters from ***s2*** to ***s1***, then return ***s1***
void *memmove(*s1* , *s2* , *n*)	same as **memcpy()** but it also works even when the objects overlap
int memcmp(*s1* , *s2* , *n*)	compare the first ***n*** characters of ***s1*** with ***s2***; return as with the **strcmp()** function
void *memchr(*s* , *c* , *n*)	return a pointer to the first occurrence of character ***c*** in ***s***, or return **NULL** if not present in the first ***n*** characters
void *memset(*s* , *c* , *n*)	place character ***c*** into the first ***n*** characters of ***s***, then return ***s***

<math.h>

Math functions

The **math.h** header file contains functions that perform mathematical calculations. All the functions are listed in the table below, together with a description of the calculation they perform. In the table ***x*** and ***y*** are double data types, and ***n*** is an **int** data type. All the functions return the result of their calculation as a **double** data type:

Function:	Description:
sin(*x*)	return the sine of ***x***
cos(*x*)	return the cosine of ***x***
tan(*x*)	return the tangent of ***x***
asin(*x*)	return the arcsine of ***x***
acos(*x*)	return the arccosine of ***x***
atan(*x*)	return the arctangent of ***x***
atan2(*y* , *x*)	return the angle (in radians) from the ***x*** axis to a point ***y***
sinh(*x*)	return the hyperbolic sine of ***x***
cosh(*x*)	return the hyperbolic cosine of ***x***
tanh(*x*)	return the hyperbolic tangent of ***x***
exp(*x*)	return e (the base of natural logarithms) raised to the power ***x***
log(*x*)	return the natural logarithm of ***x***
log10(*x*)	return the base 10 logarithm of ***x***
pow(*x* , *y*)	return ***x*** raised to the power ***y***
sqrt(*x*)	return the square root of ***x***

Function:	Description:
ceil(***x*** **)**	return the smallest integer not less than ***x*** , as a double
floor(***x*** **)**	return the largest integer not greater than ***x*** , as a double
fabs(***x*** **)**	return the absolute value of ***x***
ldexp(***x*** **,** ***n*** **)**	return ***x*** multiplied by 2 and raised to the power ***n***
frexp(***x*** **, int ****exp*** **)**	decompose ***x*** into two parts – return a mantissa between 0.5 and 1, and store exponent in ***exp***
modf(***x*** **, double ****ip*** **)**	split ***x*** into integer and fraction – return the fractional part, and store the integral part in ***ip***
fmod(***x*** **,** ***y*** **)**	return the remainder of ***x*** divided by ***y***

<stdlib.h>

Functions that perform various useful tasks

Utility functions

double atof(const char ***s*** **)** Converts ***s*** to a **double**
int atoi(const char ***s*** **)** Converts ***s*** to an **int**
long atol(const char ***s*** **)** Converts ***s*** to a **long**
double strtod(const char ***s*** **, char** ****endp*** **)** Converts the initial part of ***s*** to a **double**, ignoring leading whitespace. A pointer to the rest of ***s*** is stored in ****endp***
long strtol(const char ***s*** **, char** ****endp*, int *b*** **)** Converts the initial part of ***s*** to a **long** using base ***b***. A pointer to the rest of ***s*** is stored in ****endp***
unsigned long strtoul(const char ***s*** **, char** ****endp*** **, int** ***b*** **)** This function is the same as the **strtol()** function except the returned result is an **unsigned long**
int rand(void) Returns a pseudo-random number between zero and an implementation-defined maximum of at least 32,767
void srand(unsigned int ***seed*** **)** Sets the seed for a new sequence of random numbers supplied by **rand()**. The initial seed is 1
void *calloc(size_t ***nobj*** **, size_t** ***size*** **)** Returns a pointer to memory space for an array of ***nobj*** objects of ***size*** size, or **NULL** if the request cannot be met. The space is initialized to zero bytes
void *malloc(size_t ***size*** **)** Returns a pointer to memory space for an object of ***size*** size, or **NULL** if the request fails. This space is uninitialized
void *realloc(void ***p*** **, size_t** ***size*** **)** Changes the size of an object pointed to by ***p*** to ***size*** size. This function returns a pointer to the new space, or **NULL** if the request fails
void *free(void ***p*** **)** The **free()** function deallocates the memory space pointed to by ***p***. Note that ***p*** must be a pointer to memory space previously allocated by **calloc()**, **malloc()**, or **realloc()**

void abort(void) Causes the program to end abnormally
void exit(int *status*) Causes the program to end normally. The value of ***status*** is returned to the system. Optionally, **EXIT_SUCCESS** and **EXIT_FAILURE** can be used to specify the ***status*** values
int atexit(void (**fcn*) (void)) Registers the ***fcn*** function to be called when the program terminates. **atexit()** returns a non-zero value if unsuccessful
int system(const char **s*) Passes the string ***s*** to the environment for processing. The return value is implementation-dependent
char *getenv(const char **name*) Returns the environment string associated with ***name***, or **NULL** if no string is associated with ***name*** in that environment. The details are implementation-dependent
void *bsearch(const void **key* , const void **base* , size_t *n* , size_t *size* , int (*cmp) , (const void **keyval* , const void **datum*)) Searches ***base*[0]...*base*[*n*-1]** for an item that matches ***key***. It returns a pointer to the matching item if successful, otherwise it returns a **NULL** value. Items in the array base must be in ascending order
void qsort(void **base* , size_t *n* , size_t *size* , int (*cmp) (const void * , const void *)) Sorts into ascending order an array ***base*[0]...*base*[*n*-1]** of objects of ***size*** size. The comparison function **cmp()** is the same as that in the **bsearch()** function
int abs(int *n*) Returns the absolute value of **int *n***
long labs(long *n*) Returns the absolute value of **long *n***
div_t ldiv(long *num* , long *denom*) Divides ***num*** by ***denom*** and stores the result as members of a structure of type **ldiv_t**. Its **quot** member stores the quotient result and its **rem** member stores the remainder result

<assert.h>

Diagnostic functions

The **assert()** function, contained in the **assert.h** header file, can be used to add diagnostics to a program:

void assert(int *expression*) ;

If ***expression*** is zero when **assert(*expression*)** is executed the function will print a message on **stderr**, such as:

Assertion failed: *expression* , file *filename* , line *n*

The **assert()** function then attempts to terminate the program.

<stdarg.h>

Argument functions

The **stdarg.h** header file contains functions that can be used to step through a list of function arguments without first knowing their number and type. Due to the nature of these functions they must be implemented as "macros" within the function body.

The list of arguments is assigned to a special data type named **va_list**. The functions listed in the following table manipulate a variable named "args" of the **va_list** type:

va_start(va_list *args* , *lastarg*)
Must be called once to initialize the **va_list** named ***args*** at the position in the list of the last known argument ***lastarg***
va_arg(va_list *args* , *data-type*)
After **va_list *args*** has been initialized by **va_start()** each successive call to **va_arg()** will return the value of the next argument in the ***args*** list as the specified ***data-type***
va_end(va_list *args*)
Must be called once after the arguments in the **va_list *args*** have been processed, before the function is exited

Date & time functions

The **time.h** header file contains functions for manipulating date and time. Some of these functions process "Calendar time", which is based on the Gregorian calendar. This is stated in seconds elapsed since the Epoch (00:00:00 GMT January 1st, 1970).

Other functions contained in **time.h** process "Local time", which is the translation of Calendar time accounting for time zone.

The data type **time_t** is used to describe both Calendar time and Local time.

A struct named **tm** contains the components of Calendar time, which are listed in the table below:

Component:	Description:
int tm_sec	seconds after the minute, 0-61
int tm_min	minutes after the hour, 0-59
int tm_hour	hours since midnight, 0-23
int tm_mday	day of the month, 1-31
int tm_mon	months since January, 0-11
int tm_year	years since 1900
int tm_wday	days since Sunday, 0-6
int tm_yday	days since January 1st, 0-365
int tm_isdst	Daylight Saving Time flag

The **tm_isdst** component is positive if Daylight Saving is in effect, zero if it is not, or negative if the information is unavailable.

The functions contained in the **time.h** header file are listed in the table on page 182.

...cont'd

The **time.h** header file contains the functions listed below that can be used to manipulate date and time:

clock_t clock(void) Returns the processor time used by the program since it started, or -1 if unavailable
time_t time(time_t *tp) Returns the current calendar time, or -1 if unavailable
double difftime(time_t *time2* , time_t *time1*) Returns ***time2*** minus ***time1***, expressed in seconds
time_t mktime(struct tm *tp) Converts the local time in the structure ***tp** into calendar time
char *asctime(const struct tm *tp) Converts the time in the struct ***tp** into a standard string
char *ctime(const time_t *tp) Converts calendar time to local time
struct tm *gmtime(const time_t *tp) Converts calendar time into Co-ordinated Universal Time (UTC or GMT)
struct tm *localtime(const time_t *tp) Converts the calendar time ***tp** into local time
size_t strftime(char *s , size_t smax , const char *fmt , const struct tm *tp) Formats the time ***tp** into a chosen format *fmt

The **strftime()** function formats selected components of the **tm** structure according to the stated format specifier. All the possible format specifiers are listed in the table on the opposite page.

Specifier:	Description:
%a	abbreviated weekday name
%A	full weekday name
%b	abbreviated month name
%B	full month name
%c	local date and time representation
%d	day of the month, 01-31
%H	hour (24-hour clock), 00-23
%I	hour (12-hour clock), 01-12
%j	day of the year, 001-366
%m	month of the year, 01-12
%M	minute, 00-59
%p	local equivalent of AM or PM
%S	second, 00-61 (to account for leap seconds)
%U	week number of the year (Sunday as the first day of the week), 00-53
%w	weekday number, 0-6 (Sunday is 0)
%W	week number of the year (Monday as the first day of the week), 00-53
%x	local date representation
%X	local time representation
%y	year without century, 00-99
%Y	year with century
%Z	time zone name, if available

<setjmp.h>

Jump functions

The **setjmp.h** header is used for controlling low-level calls and provides a means to avoid the normal call and return sequence.

int setjmp(jmp_buf *env*)
Low-level function used in conditional tests to save the environment in the ***env*** variable, then return zero
void longjmp(jmp_buf *env* , int *value*)
Restores an environment that has been saved in the ***env*** variable by **setjmp()**, as if **setjmp()** had returned the ***value***

<signal.h>

Signal functions

The **signal.h** header contains functions for handling exceptional conditions that may arise during the execution of a program:

void (*signal (int *sig* , void (**handler*) (int))) (int)
The **signal()** function specifies how subsequent signals will be handled. The handler can be **SIG_DFL**, an implementation-defined default; or **SIG_IGN**, to ignore the signal. Valid ***sig*** signals include:

SIGABRT : abort termination
SIGFPE : arithmetic error
SIGILL : illegal instruction
SIGINT : external interruption
SIGSEGV : access outside memory limit
SIGTERM : termination request sent to the program

The function returns the previous value of the handler for that specific signal, or **SIG_ERR** if an error occurs. When a ***sig*** signal next occurs, the signal is restored to its default behavior then the signal handler is called. If this returns, execution resumes at the point where the signal occurred

int raise(int *sig*)
Attempts to send the ***sig*** signal to the program and returns a non-zero value if the attempt is unsuccessful

Limit constants

The table below lists constants related to maximum and minimum numerical limits. Their values vary according to implementation. Where a value is given, in brackets, it indicates a minimum size for that constant – but larger values may, in fact, be imposed. Programs should not assume that any implementation-dependent constant will be of a particular value.

Constant:	Value:
CHAR_BIT	number of bits in a **char** (8)
CHAR_MAX	maximum value of **char** (**UCHAR_MAX** or **SCHAR_MAX**)
CHAR_MIN	minimum value of char (zero or **SCHAR_MIN**)
INT_MAX	maximum value of **int** (+32,767)
INT_MIN	minimum value of **int** (-32,767)
LONG_MAX	maximum value of **long** (+2,147,483,647)
LONG_MIN	minimum value of **long** (-2,147,483,647)
SCHAR_MAX	maximum value of **signed char** (+127)
SCHAR_MIN	minimum value of **signed char** (-127)
SHRT_MAX	maximum value of **short** (+32,767)
SHRT_MIN	minimum value of **short** (-32,767)
UCHAR_MAX	maximum value of **unsigned char** (+255)
UINT_MAX	maximum value of **unsigned int** (+65,535)
ULONG_MAX	maximum value of **unsigned long** (+4,294,967,295)
USHRT_MAX	maximum value of **unsigned short** (+65, 535)

Float constants

The table below lists constants related to floating-point arithmetic. Their values vary according to implementation. Where a value is given, in brackets, it indicates a minimum size for that constant.

Constant:	Value:
FLT_RADIX	radix of float exponent representations (2)
FLT_ROUNDS	rounding to the nearest number
FLT_DIG	number of precision digits (5)
FLT_EPSILON	smallest number x, where 1.0 + x != 1.0 (1E-5)
FLT_MANT_DIG	number of **FLT_RADIX** mantissa digits
FLT_MAX	maximum floating-point number (1E+37)
FLT_MAX_EXP	largest number n, where **FLT_RADIX**^{n}-1 is a valid number
FLT_MIN	minimum floating-point number (1E-37)
FLT_MIN_EXP	smallest number n, where 10^{n} is valid
DBL_DIG	number of double-precision digits (10)
DBL_EPSILON	smallest number x, where 1.0 + x != 1.0 (1E-9)
DBL_MANT_DIG	number of **FLT_RADIX** mantissa digits
DBL_MAX	maximum double float number (1E+37)
DBL_MAX_EXP	largest number n, where **FLT_RADIX**^{n}-1 is a valid number
DBL_MIN	minimum double float number (1E-37)
DBL_MIN_EXP	smallest number n, where 10^{n} is valid

Index

A

abort() function 179
abs() function 179
accessibility 28
  restricting 94
access time 30
acos() function 176
addition operator + 52
addressof operator & 24, 98
American National Standards Institute (ANSI) 8
AND operator && 58
angled brackets < > 12
appending text to a file 144
arguments 88
arithmetic operators 52
  +, /, -, *, % 52
array
  index 36
  pointers 104
  variables 34
arrow operator -> 130
ASCII code values 32, 162-163
asctime() function 152, 182
asin() function 176
assembler conversion 16
Assembly language files .s 16
assert() function 180
assert.h header file 9, 180
assignment operators
  =, +=, -=, *=, /=, %= 54
associativity precedence 68
asterisk character * 41
atan2() function 176
atan() function 176
atexit() function 179
atof() function 178
atoi() function 120, 178
atol() function 178
auto keyword 28

B

binary number 64
bit flag manipulation 66-67
bitwise operators
  & AND, | OR, ~ NOT, ^ XOR
    << Shift left, >> Shift right 64
boolean values
  true (1), false (0) 58
braces { } 12
break keyword 74, 80
bsearch() function 179
byte, 8 bits 64

C

Calendar time 152
calloc() function 136, 178
case keyword 74
casting data types 32
ceil() function 177
character array 110
character format specifier %c 22
character pointer 128
char data type
  char keyword 21
clearerr() function 171
C libraries 9
clock() function 154, 182
comments 21
comparison operators
  ==, !=, >, <, >=, <= 56
compilation process 14-17
compiler 10-11
  -mwindows option 158
  -o option 14
  -save-temps option 17
  translation 16
conditional branching
  case, break, default, switch keywords 74
  if, else keywords 72
conditional operator ?: 60
constants
  const keyword 40

continue keyword 81
correct single/plural grammar 60
cos() function 176
cosh() function 176
ctime() function 182
ctype.h header file 9, 118, 173
custom data types 44

D

data type conversion
  casting 32
data types
  char, int, float, double 21
  int 13
date and time
  tm struct components 152
date and time format specifiers 183
debugging source code 48
decrement operator -- 52
default statement
  default keyword 74
dereference operator * 98
dereferencing pointers 98
dialog box 158
difftime() function 154, 182
division operator / 52
dot operator . 124, 126
double data type
  double keyword 21
do while loop 76, 78
  do, while keywords 76, 78

E

elements array 34
else keyword 72
enum data type
  enum keyword 44
enumerating constants
  enum keyword 42
EOF constant 143, 144
Epoch 152
equality operator == 56, 116
errno.h header file 150
errors
  reporting 150
exit() function 179
exp() function 176
external global variable
  extern keyword 28

F

fabs() function 177
false value (0) 58
fclose() function 140, 165
feof() function 149, 170, 171
ferror() function 170, 171
fflush() function 164
fgetc() function 142, 169
fgetpos() function 172
fgets() function 110, 142, 144, 169
file 140
  modes
    r, w, a, r+, w+, a+ 140
  open, read, write, close 140
  pointer 140
  read and write entire filestreams 142, 146
  reading and writing characters 142
  reading and writing lines 142, 144
FILE data type 140
filestream 142
  nominating 148
flag values 66
float constants 186
float data type
  float keyword 21
float.h header file 9, 186
floating-point arithmetic 32
floating-point format specifier %f 22
floor() function 177
fmod() function 177
fopen() function 140, 164
for loop
  for keyword 76
formal parameters 88
format specifiers
  %d, %ld, %f, %c, %s, %p 22
  for input 168
  for output 167
fprintf() function 142, 148, 166
fputc() function 142, 169
fputs() function 142, 144, 169
fread() function 142, 146, 170

free() function 136, 178
freopen() function 164
frexp() function 177
fscanf() function 142, 148, 166
fseek() function 172
fsetpos() function 172
ftell() function 172
function 12, 86
  arguments 12, 88
  declaration, prototype 86
  definition 86
  header file 92
  pointers 106
  recursive 90
  static 94
  syntax 12
fwrite() function 142, 146, 170

G

General Public License (GPL) 10
getc() function 169
getchar() function 169
getenv() function 179
global variables 28
gmtime() function 182
GNU C Compiler (GCC) 10
goto keyword 82
greater than operators
  >, >= 56

H

hash character # 12
header files 9
  custom 92
Hello World program 12

I

if else statement
  if keyword 72
increment operator ++ 52
indirection operator * 98
inequality operator != 56, 116
initializing arrays 34
initializing variables 21
input 24
int data type
  int keyword 13, 21
integer format specifier %d 22
isalnum() function 173
isalpha() function 118, 173
iscntrl() function 173
isdigit() function 118, 173
isgraph() function 173
islower() function 118, 173
isprint() function 173
ispunct() function 118, 173
isspace() function 118, 173
isupper() function 118, 173
isxdigit() function 173
iteration loop 76
itoa() function 120

L

labs() function 179
ldexp() function 177
ldiv() function 179
Least Significant Bit (LSB) 64
less than operators
  <, <= 56
limit constants 185
limits.h header file 9, 26, 185
linker combination 16
Linux platform
  linux constant 46
  malloc_usable_size() function 136
localtime() function 152, 182
local variables 28
log10() function 176
log() function 176
logical operators
  && AND, || OR, ! NOT 58
longjmp() function 184
long qualifier
  long keyword 26
loop structures
  break statement 80
  continue statement 81
  for, while, do while loops 76
  goto statement 82
L-value 128

M

macro preprocessor routine 46
main() function 12
malloc() function 136, 178
math.h header file 9, 176
members 124
memchr() function 175
memcmp() function 175
memcpy() function 175
memmove() function 175
memory 24
memory address 98
memory address format specifier %p 22
memory allocation 136
memory size 62
memset() function 175
Minimalist GNU for Windows (MinGW) 10
mktime() function 182
modf() function 177
modulus operator % 52
Most Significant Bit (MSB) 64
multi-dimensional arrays 36
multiplication operator * 52

N

naming conventions 20
nested loop 77
newline character 144
newline escape sequence \n 13
NOT operator ! 58
null character \0 34, 110
NULL value 116, 136, 140

O

object files .o 16
operand 52
operator precedence 68
operators
  arithmetical +, -, *, /, %, ++, -- 52
  assignment =, +=, -=, *=, /=, %= 54
  bitwise &, |, ~, ^, <<, >> 64
  comparison ==, !=, >, <, >=, <= 56
  conditional ? : 60
  logical &&, ||, ! 58
  precedence rules 68
  sizeof 62
OR operator || 58

P

parentheses () 12, 32, 62, 106
parity evaluation 61
passing data
  by value, by reference 88, 132
perror() function 150, 171
pointer
  arguments 102
  arithmetic 100
  array 104
  in a structure 128
  to a function 106
  to a struct member -> 130
  to a structure 130
  to a union 134
  variables 98
postfix position 52
pow() function 176
precedence 68
precision specifier 22
prefix position 52
preprocessor directives 12
  #define 46
  #elif 48
  #else 48
  #endif 46
  #if 48
  #ifdef 46
  #ifndef 48
  #include 12, 16, 92
  #undef 48
preprocessor substitution 16
printf() function 13, 22, 166
putc() function 169
putchar() function 169
puts() function 110, 169

Q

qsort() function 179
qualifiers
  long, short, unsigned 26
quotes 110
R-value 128

R

raise() function 184
rand() function 156, 178
random numbers 156
realloc() function 136, 178
recursive functions 90
register variables
  register keyword 30
remove() function 165
rename() function 165
return value 86
  return keyword 13
R-value 128

S

scanf() function 24, 110, 166
semi-colon terminator 12
setbuf() function 165
setjmp() function 184
setjmp.h header file 9, 184
setvbuf() function 165
short qualifier
  short keyword 26
signal() function 184
signal.h header file 9, 184
signed values
  signed keyword 26
sin() function 176
sinh() function 176
sizeof operator 62, 110
  sizeof keyword 26
sprintf() function 120, 166
sqrt() function 176
srand() function 156, 178
sscanf() function 166
standard C libraries 9
static keyword 28, 94
stdarg.h header file 9, 180
stderr messages 142
stdin, keyboard 142, 148
stdio.h header file 9, 140, 164
stdlib.h header file 9, 120, 136, 156, 178
stdout, monitor 142, 148
strcat() function 114, 174
strchr() function 117, 174
strcmp() function 116, 174
strcpy() function 112, 174
strcspn() function 174
strerror() function 150, 175
strftime() function 152, 182
string
  comparison 116
  length 112
string format specifier %s 22
string.h header 150
string.h header file 9, 112, 174
strings 34, 104
  concatenating, joining 114
  converting 120
  copying 112
  finding substrings 116
  reading 110
  validating 118
strings " " 13
strlen() function 112, 175
strncat() function 114, 174
strncmp() function 174
strncpy() function 112, 174
strpbrk() function 175
strrchr() function 117, 174
strspn() function 174
strstr() function 116, 175
strtod() function 178
strtok() function 175
strtol() function 178
strtoul() function 178
structures
  as data type 126
  passing as arguments 132
  struct keyword 63, 124
subtraction operator - 52
switch statement
  switch keyword 74
system() function 179

T

tab escape sequence \t 27
tag names 124
capitalize 126
tan() function 176
tanh() function 176
temporary files 17
ternary operator ?: 60
time() function 182
time.h header file 9, 152, 154, 181
time(NULL) function 152
timer 154
time_t data type 152, 154
tmpfile() function 165
tmpnam() function 165
tm struct 152
tm struct components 181
tolower() function 118, 173
toupper() function 118, 173
true value (1) 58
type definition
typedef keyword 44, 126

U

unary operator 58
ungetc() function 169
union keyword 134
unsigned qualifier
unsigned keyword 26
uppercase constant names 40

V

va_arg() function 180
va_end() function 180
variable 20
variable arrays 34
variable scope 28
va_start() function 180
void keyword 86
volatile keyword 30
vprintf(), vfprintf(), vsprintf() functions 166

W

while loop 76, 78
Windows Application Programming Interface (WINAPI) 158
Windows platform
MessageBox() function 158
_msize() function 136
_WIN32 constant 46
windows.h header file 158
WinMain() function 158

Z

zero-based index 36